DEVOURING BIRDS

Printed in the United States of America

ISBN 978-0-646-57982-5

Grateful acknowledgement is made to the editors of the following journals and books where many of these poems first appeared:

Asylum, Aquarian Weekly, Carnival, Chiron Review, Chronogram Magazine, Clark Street Review, Concrete Meat Press, Fly Paper Press, Green Mountain Review, Kamini Press, Kendra Steiner Editions, Laura Hird, Literature and its Writers/Bedford St.Martin's Press, Modern English Tanka, Metropolis, Pearl, Poetry Dispatch, Thunder Sandwich, Tideline Press, Woodstock Times, Wormwood Review, Yellow Silk, Zerx Press.

Front cover photograph taken by Ronald Baatz from the porch of Thomas Cole's house in Catskill, New York.

for Marvin Malone

"... even during the war the sparrows did not really grow thinner.
Even then there was plenty of dirt in the streets of Trieste for them to feed on."

Italo Svevo

DEVOURING BIRDS

New and Selected Poems

Ronald Baatz

Blind Dog Press

Australia

Table of Contents

IN COMMON

A sparrow flies from the shed to the garden.
It is a very short distance, one which
I have often walked while carrying a rake.
What I have in common with the rake
is that we both have teeth.
What I have in common with the sparrow
is that we both could perish at any second.
I admire the rake's durability.
I admire the sparrow's song.

THE WEIGHT OF THE SWIMMER

Just a few weeks ago the woods were different.
  Because of snow they were almost impossible
to enter without snowshoes on. Now there is
  so much green that the sky at sunrise is strictly
a vainglorious yellow. It's June, and already
  I look forward to summer falling to its knees,
dying in wind that has nothing worth mentioning
  except the cold. As with the endless
sentences I speak internally, I wish the green
  would perish and once again there would be
a quiet starkness. Life is everywhere,
  crowding, pushing, killing, eating, multiplying.
In the city there are the throngs of people.
  In the country it is the green, the incalculable
wealth of leaves of every shape, accruing,
  curving, stretching. Even the wall, down
at the dam, is covered with ivy.
  Swimming there this morning, we talked
about a recent drowning.
  It seems that when the ivy is grabbed,
it almost always breaks from
  the weight of the swimmer.

LATE AT NIGHT

Late at night I drive out to the gas station,
   the one that is little more than a shack
located on the narrow highway at the edge of town.
   When I pull up, slowly in fresh snow,
I notice a string of tiny white Christmas lights
   in the large window facing the pumps.
Because these lights burn with such resolve,
   I jump to the conclusion that someone
must be inside. I'm in search of the
   comfort found in taking a drive alone at night,
simply to pick up a bag of peanuts
   to eat on the way home. But when I try
to open the door I find it locked, and when
   I look through the window I see no one
stirring inside. A green banker's lamp
   is on a desk, lighting piles of grimy papers.
So, I get back in the car intending
   to continue my search, but before I do so
I sit for a while, maneuvring
   a cough drop around in my mouth, my tongue
careful not to cut itself on the sharp edge.
   I stare at the lights loosely framing the window
that is gray with soot. The snow
   keeps coming down gently, as though
it were afraid of doing something wrong.
   When I yawn,
my breath floats
   free of the car.

THE STUFF MY DREAMS ARE MADE OF

With a lot of other stuff, the couch put out at the curb
for the garbage truck is soaking up rain as fast as
the rain is falling. I thought the truck would've been
here by now. The couch has been out for three days.
I hope the rain doesn't make it too heavy to pick up.
This same couch was in one of my dreams last night.
I was dragging it, in this gray drizzly dream, through
a narrow street to a friend's apartment. As I
made my way the couch got stuck in every crack,
on every bump. People were standing around watching,
giggling, talking under their breath. And in this dream,
this gray drizzly dream, children who came out
of nowhere wanted to play on it. Wildly they
jumped up and down, yelling and screaming, teasing
one another, calling me every imaginable silly name.
When I could go on no farther, I sat down on the couch
among the children who were multiplying like flies.
They paid little attention to me, treating me as though
I were just another cushion. It wasn't long before
I couldn't take it anymore and I started screaming,
sending children scurrying in every direction. Once
I reached my friend's apartment we dragged the couch
up to the fourth floor. We shoved the decrepit
looking thing up against the wall opposite a TV gray
with dust. He handed me a pink lemonade and we sat
drinking while the TV was warming up. When
the picture came on, all it consisted of was a naked
light bulb hanging from a wire, burning like the
fireplace scene broadcast at Christmastime.
We sat sipping, watching, not saying a word.
It was such a dreary, drizzly gray dream, the kind
I'm all too familiar with. As I try to reconstruct
what happened next in the dream, I stare out
the front window at the couch, which is still soaking
up rain. Perhaps tonight I will dream about
the garbage truck. In the rain a small child walks by,
hands in pockets, hair drenched, completely
ignoring the stuff my dreams are made of.

THE CICADAS

The cicadas are making a racket tonight.
God only knows how many of them are
out there. You cannot hear yourself think.
Earlier, when I was standing outside I felt
totally engulfed by this racket as the sky,
without thunder, periodically flashed white.
Now there is also the sound of thunder
marching closer and closer to the house, so I
shut the air-conditioner off and open a window.
I pace, light a thin cigar, watch the smoke
slowly making its way towards the window.
When the smoke disappears through the screen
I take another puff and start the journey of smoke
all over again. Once overhead, the storm
comes crashing down without mercy. Curious
to know how this might be affecting the cicadas,
I put my head up close to the screen. They're quiet.
Quiet as scared humans, they are.

THE WAITRESS

I play with a green ashtray while watching the cook put muscle
into scrubbing the grill with a brush. He drags on a cigarette
loosely hanging from his lips, ashes falling and disappearing
on the way down. When the waitress brings more coffee
I ask her how close we are to closing time and she tells me,
"We're almost there, darling." I was in earlier for dinner
and we had talked the usual talk, but this time when
I was pushing my plate away I ventured to invite her
out after her shift was over. I think my asking came
as a surprise to both of us. Often I have daydreamed
about being with her. She knows I'm broke, so
no effort will be made to impress her. Leaving,
we hear the owner yelling at the top of his voice,
reminding her that she has to open in the morning.
In the street we exchange vague smiles. After all the meals
she has served me we are still complete strangers.
Her dark eyes are beautiful and in their expression
I can see a weariness that somehow has managed to
remain serene. When we reach my place we throw
our coats on the couch. She sits down on them and
I fetch a bottle of wine and open it on the coffee table
in front of her, a little embarrassed at there being no cork.
The night passes. Towards the end of the third bottle
we laugh with pure abandon, our kisses getting sloppy
and passionate. I can smell the diner on her. I can say
that it's a wonderful perfume. I refuse to let her shower.
My, how butter does melt in a baked potato. In the morning
I hear the alarm go off, but before I can prop myself up on
my elbows she drops her turquoise uniform over her head.
Without a mirror she combs her hair back, then shoves her
pocketbook under her arm and approaches the bed.
She places her hand on my forehead as though checking
to see if I am running a fever. She gives me a peck on
the cheek and reminds me that today is Wednesday, and
Wednesday's special is pot roast.

MOVING TO THE DESERT

I cannot live here when I am old.
   It is too cold for many months out of the year.
   As it is, I am having a rough time dealing with
the cold now. When I am old I want to live
   in the desert. I suppose this is a common goal
   for people who live in the cold. Although, thankfully,
this past winter was a blessing, so unbelievably mild was it.
   The morning newspaper explains why
   there is such an abundance of yellowjackets.
I was stung recently. I was sitting on the green lawn chair
   at the back of the house, minding my own business, reading,
   when suddenly I felt an itch on my leg. As I scratched this itch,
one of these yellowjackets let me have it. It had managed to crawl
   up my leg, underneath my pants. After stinging me
   it fell to the ground and walked away; for some reason not flying,
perhaps too exhausted from having stung me.
   My first instinct was to kill it; instead I just moved away from it.
   I will leave these heavenly purple mountains to the bugs and the bears
and whatever else wants to claim them as their own.
   I do not want to be exposed to such cold when I am old.
   I want to bake in the sun. I want to be like a dried fig.
If I had money, then living here would not be such a hardship.
   I'd be able to defend myself from the cold with money.
   But there is none, and there appears to be nothing I can do
to rectify this problem. I live where the winters are harsh and
   I have no way of keeping myself warm. I am profoundly disappointed
   in myself. I will not even have the money necessary to move
to the desert when the time comes. So why do I even talk about it,
   dream about it. I have been pathetic at creating a decent income.
   I will die in this lousy cold. I can see it all now: when I die
others will come to take my body away, my belongings.
   They will make a thorough search of my room for money
   that I might have hidden away, and they will find not a dime.
Then they will unearth thousands
   of poems, and they will know why.

SMOKE RISING

That house burned to the ground
when there was no one home. Smoke rising
from the woods gave the fire away.
At least it appeared to be rising
from the woods, as it clouded over
the orange sun that was setting in the trees.
By the time the men arrived to put the fire out
there was almost nothing to save.
Perhaps some geese flying overhead
had seen the flames. Some of the
most beautiful wallpaper in the county
was lost in that fire.

A WALK IN THE GARDEN

I take a walk in the garden with my father, very slowly
since he is losing control of his body. Before Alzheimer's
got the best of him his body looked rugged and indestructible.
Now he wears a scowl from trying to make sense out of things
and talking in wide, painful circles. He stops in his tracks, hands
stuffed in his overcoat pockets, and he looks deep into my eyes
and begs me to tell him if I have been hiding anything from him.
He weeps like a child in an old man's body. He is a child
in an old man's body. He fears causing my mother pain.
At the far end of the yard where his garden equipment
is stored in a shed, he spots the two orange cats lying on
the picnic table. His face brightens when he pets them,
his big hand pressing their ears down so that they pop up.
He says that he would never let anyone harm them, that he would
allow himself to be killed first. Then he turns to me and asks why
I've never told him that the woman he is married to is my mother.
It makes him sad that I have kept this a secret for all these years.
His hands tremble. He says he loves my mother, that if another
man ever tried to take her away he'd knock the guy's block off.

THE ONLY EXIT

Mars is orange on this snowy autumn night, and a dog is
chasing my car through town as I grow tired of driving.
Fortunately, in front of a row of cabins I spot a vacancy sign.
The price is a mere twenty dollars a night. I can't resist.
I'm a born sucker for such accommodations. Perhaps
I'll stay more than one night, and for the time I am here
I'll get to enjoy living in this tiny settlement where life
is easy to understand and death almost never occurs.
I pull into the parking lot where two young girls are doing
cartwheels through water spraying up from a sprinkler and
a puppy is chewing on a naked doll by the swimming pool.
Something I do not care for, though, about such places, is
the tendency to use yellow bulbs on the porches, whatever
the time of year. It's unnerving to see snow in yellow light.
I ask the woman in the office if she could put a white bulb
above the door of the cabin I'll be in, and the only response
I get is a suspicious glance. The cabin smells from Lysol, so
I throw a window open and allow the cold air to circulate.
I put my suitcase on the bed. It's almost empty. I own
precious little in the way of clothing. Whatever laundry I create
I wash in sinks in motel rooms. Space is at
a premium here. There are tea bags, packets of coffee,
sugar and powdered milk on the counter next to a mug. In the
sink there is a terracotta stain created by dripping water.
Actually, it's quite beautiful and it reminds me of Mexico.
I touch it. It is icy cold. Also, I notice that every time
the refrigerator comes on, its thick black wire jumps like a frog.
There is no home, no lover and no job waiting for me at
my destination. I did this to myself. I put myself on this road.
I fear what is terrible and I leave others alone. I will sleep
tonight in a cabin that has a yellow bulb burning in the snowy
darkness. It's burning over my door, the door that is the only
entrance, the only exit.

ENVYING THE CROWS

A cold winter day spent
reading, collecting tinder.
But, my god, the loneliness
of the hours was overwhelming.
With age it becomes more and
more apparent that I need to be
among people. I have to stop living
like a monk. Although, it is true,
monks do live with other monks.
They pray, take their meals together,
and perhaps life at the monastery
is not such a burden. I would never
have to eat alone in such a place.
Earlier, I stood eating a can of sardines
and a piece of unbuttered bread.
I envied the crows. From the
kitchen window I had seen them pecking
at the leftover rice I had thrown out.
The crows, that had arrived in a group
and that had left in a group.
Same as the sardines.

OUT OF HIS CHILDHOOD

Tonight I had take-out Chinese with my parents.
My father almost choked on a tough piece of lobster.
Then he ate not only the fortune cookies but the little
white slips of paper on which the fortunes are printed
in red. My mother just sat there rolling her eyeballs,
rolling them up into her small skull. Both of them
have small skulls now. My father talked about
his garden, about what a jungle it had become.
Whenever he talks now, he seems to be staring
out of his childhood.

THE WIND AGES ME

The wind moves
through the grass.
The wind ages me.
The rain drips from
the house.
The rain ages me.
Sleep breathes deeply.
Sleep ages me.
A young woman
on a bicycle
yells to me,
"Get out of the way,
old man."
She laughs and
waves to me
as she goes by.
The moon cannot
burn a tree down.
It cannot eat
a cow or cook
a shrimp. But
it ages me.

FISH MOUTH BLUES

The old landlord knocks
at the back door and gives
me a trout. Every summer
he has the pond stocked
with about fifty trout, and
then he fishes them out.
The one he hands me is in
a plastic bag from a pharmacy.
Since he knows I don't gut fish
he has taken care of this chore.
And since he doesn't eat fish
we will not have dinner together.
Many nights we do share a meal,
usually in the barn where
he lives during the summer.
I put the fish in the big black iron
frying pan, a potato in the
microwave. I make a simple salad.
On the salad I pour some
ranch dressing that's been
in the fridge since Christmas.
Everything seems to be coming
together nicely, until I try closing
the fish's mouth.

SOMEONE ELSE

In the introduction to his autobiography
Simenon says that all writing is little more
than just a lot of chatter. This revelation
simply tempts me to close the book without
reading another word. I see him dictating
these words to his secretary while lounging
on a couch, fully dressed but with no shoes on.
Also he tells his secretary about his love affair
with Josephine Baker, but he doesn't go to any
great lengths since he is not all that sure how he
actually felt about her. At times he remembers her
with complete fondness, and at others he cannot
understand how he could ever have been attracted
to her. He thinks he remembers her having big feet,
but then realizes that he might be mixing her up with
someone else.

AT SEVEN

My father was seven when both of his parents died.
It was at this point in his life that the decision was made
that he should live with his aunt and his uncle. To this day
he'll complain that he was never treated as well as his cousins,
three very pretty girls and the oldest being a boy who looked like
a small version of Babe Ruth. My father worked on his
uncle's bread wagon for long, hard hours and in all kinds
of bad weather. He does not recall his male cousin ever
having to do any such work. Never given enough to eat,
my father was reduced to stealing bread. He would take
a loaf out of its package, when his uncle was making one
of his many tavern stops, and eat the centers of the middle slices.
Before his uncle would resurface, my father would put
the loaf back together again, hiding the fact that some
of the bread was missing, and praying that no one
in the world would ever complain.

WAITING

In the early 1900's a tavern owned by my grandfather
in Newark, New Jersey, appropriately and simply enough
was called Baatz's Tavern. Greeting you at the door
was a long, elegant bar overflowing with hot food, like
clam chowder soup and raw oysters, that you could eat
for free as you happily drank away the hours of a bitter life.
Beyond the bar was a family dining room, and beyond that
a small bowling alley where my father was to have his
very first job as a pin boy. His mother ran the kitchen
with an iron fist, while his father orchestrated the bar.
Only recently were we told that his father helped slaughter
the occasional pig in the yard out back of the tavern.
It seems he either tells a story exactly as he has told it
countless times before or he'll throw in some new details or
digressions that take us all by surprise. Frequently
one of his stories will make it quite apparent that his parents
never did have much time for him. It was not unusual
for my father to spend a day in a neighborhood movie theater.
When his parents wanted to summon him they would
call the theater. The owner would then get up on stage
and point to my father and tell him it was time to go home.
My father will tell you that this was always a source of great
pride and joy for him. When I happen to catch him sitting in
front of the television, when an old movie has him in a trance,
I'll wonder if in his subconscious being he is waiting for
the owner of the theater to again get up on stage to tell him
that it is time to go home. I'll wonder if my father is waiting
to be told to go home to that brief period of happiness
in his childhood, that period before becoming an orphan
for the rest of his life, before his young mother died of cancer
and his young father died from drinking because of the cancer.

A SMALL POEM IN WHICH SOCRATES, MOZART, MATISSE, CHEKHOV AND EINSTEIN ARE ALL SQUEEZED IN

Poor old Socrates had so few geniuses in history
to keep him company. He never had Mozart's
piano music to listen to. He never had Matisse's
colorful observations to find pleasure gazing at.
He never had Chekhov's letters to read, one
in which he mentions enjoying a bowl of rich
sorrel soup in a train station. None of this was
available to him to help take his mind off matters.
We know this is not true of Einstein. We know
that he loved Mozart. But god only knows what
precious thoughts went through that brain of his
while listening. Perhaps, one evening, he thought
about the lovely young woman he had seen while
walking across campus lost in thought,
flakes of snow coming to rest in his hair
like the tiniest of birds, chirpless and blind.

ONE DAY

The horse pulling the bread wagon came to a standstill
on the railroad tracks. It was summer, a boiling hot day,
the city was fiercely going about its business and everything
under the sun was attempted to get the horse to move. But
the dumb animal remained determined in its stubbornness
not to take another step. Finally, his patience exhausted,
my father's uncle rolled up a newspaper, put a lit match to it
and then placed the burning newspaper under the horse's belly,
and with that the problem was eliminated. Obligingly,
the horse stepped off the tracks. It had been a frightening ordeal,
my father will say, but not quite as frightening as the time he gave
the very same horse an apple to eat. Instead of taking hold
of the apple the horse took hold of my father's hand, and it was a
very firm hold and the horse had no intentions of letting go.
My father (usually making a fist at this point in the story)
then struck the horse with all the might of his free hand,
almost knocking the poor animal off its feet. This
allowed him to free his hand. And from that day forward,
he liked to take pleasure in reminding a person that,
because of this experience, he was far less intimidated by
the cruel world in which he was forced to survive.

SATURDAY MORNING

It's early on a Saturday morning when my shoes drag
damp autumn leaves into the kitchen of my parents' house.
My father is still sleeping. My mother is at the kitchen sink
putting water in the coffee pot. Most of the soft gray light
coming in the window settles in her hair. After we put away
the groceries I brought with me, my mother begins to get
breakfast together. Eventually my father makes his entrance.
With eyes like a turtle he slowly makes a path towards
the island where he can sit and gaze outside while eating
his egg sandwich. He looks at me, not knowing who I am.
I have to explain that I am his son. He takes a closer look,
then claims that I am my mother's brother, Uncle Mike.
I remind him that Uncle Mike is dead. My father says,
"Again?"

BUTTERNUT SQUASH

When my father was a healthy man his garden would produce
more vegetables than any family could ever imagine consuming.
I'd take bags and bags home, which I would share with neighbors
and friends. Everyone was thankful, but after awhile they seemed
to just expect them. Although, where I work, there is this woman
who, to this day, still talks about the wonderful butternut squash
that I had given to her. She and her husband added it to an array
of tasty dishes. But since I have none to give her this year,
I'll probably end up buying squash at a produce stand and
telling her that it is from my father's garden.   Last year,
as a measure of thanks, she gave me a bottle of red wine at
Halloween. She said it was one of her husband's favorites.
It wasn't a cheap wine, I could tell that much. I took it over to
my parents' house to share it with them. My father appreciated it,
very much so, especially after he had mixed in what he considered
to be the proper amount of ginger ale.

UGLY SHIRTS

i got a big tear in
my shirt but since it
is a shirt with an ugly

pattern i threw it away
and this morning when
i did this i noticed in

the trash can another
shirt with an ugly pattern
that has a tear in it that

i had thrown away yesterday
so that's two ugly shirts
in two days that have

gone out of my life if i can
say that with any conviction
because really they have not

gone out of my life at all
since when i think of my
life i am forced to admit

that the trash can certainly is
part of it and whatever is in
the trash can is likewise part

of what i must consider my life
so two ugly shirts are there in
the trash can with coffee

grounds thrown over them
reminding me that i am now
two shirts closer to having no

shirts and that i am a person
who has no qualms about even
wearing an ugly shirt once i

have been given one and that
i am a person people like
to give ugly shirts to

and that i am a person who has
people in his life who know exactly
what constitutes an ugly shirt and

where such a shirt can be found in
a world overflowing with shirts
they know i am the person who

will wear an ugly shirt until
it tears across my back as
though lashed by a whip

fiercely set into motion by
the passing of the years
also very ugly.

IN THE GARDEN IN THE WINTERTIME

We are not to argue with my father. We are not to correct any of the crazy things he might come out with. I have no problem agreeing with this, since all my life it seems I've been trying to avoid disagreements and confrontations with him. I tell him that we are planning a big birthday party for him this year, but he doesn't seem to care. There's a twinkle in his eye, though, when he tells me that he is going to ask my mother if she will marry him, this after being married for over sixty years.
I agree that it's a good idea, that he shouldn't let such a beauty slip through his fingers. And with that he looks at his leathery, dark, knobby hands and slowly he rubs them together.
He wonders, out loud, if worms freeze in the garden in the wintertime.

THE HORSE WITH THE GREEN WINGS

My mother tells me that two nights ago my father got up
in the middle of the night, dressed and put a comb and
a lamp into a suitcase. Then he woke my mother to
tell her to get ready to leave, that they were going to return
to the house on River Road, where they haven't lived
in more than twenty years. While making me an egg sandwich
she tells me this. Also I should know that my father had seen a
horse with green wings on the road out front. Later,
while we are having dinner, he sits staring, every so often making
a comment that has nothing to do with what we are
talking about. At one point he says, "Men like to start
fights and demolish cities." We are always amazed when he speaks
some indisputable truth. His appetite is good, and
when my mother gives him a Klondike Bar his face lights up like an
amusement park. Every night he devours one but
never fails to act as though it is the first time ever
that he's had ice cream. Swallowing the last bite, he wraps his arms
around himself and shivers. Then announces that the house is cold
and that he's going to go down
into the basement to start a fire.

GAIL WORE NYLONS

We met at a Halloween party. We were in 7th grade and playing
  Spin the Bottle. When I spun it, it stopped and pointed with a dreamy,
  abrupt accuracy at Gail. She was a beautiful little Italian girl who
was very round and very ivory. We disappeared in a dark secluded room
  where we kissed, where we fell in love (as much as you can fall in love
  at that age). And in love we stayed, at least till the school year was over.
After that, we drifted apart like two leaves falling deep in the woods.
  When she started swimming at the town pool she would ask me to
  meet her there but, unable to swim and scrawny as a homeless dog,
I refused. I feared the other boys mercilessly ribbing me and
  even trying to drown me. Or I feared being pushed into an
  empty pool and shattering at the bottom like a delicate tea cup.
I was oversensitive and very insecure (a poet, but as yet unaware
  of this calling). Overall, I thought of myself as being a cool kid.
  I combed my hair like Ricky Nelson, looked convincingly dashing
in my boy scout uniform. I was smart enough not to tell a soul that
  I was a bookworm. For that year that we were lovers, we either talked
  on the phone or wrote love letters or endlessly made out
like unhinged eccentric love birds having no tomorrow.
  We never actually made love, which only caused our experience
  to be one of perpetually unfulfilled desire. Every Saturday
we would go to the local theater and neck through two movies.
  There was a clock to the left of the screen. Its
  numbers and hands glowed a spooky suggestive purple, as did
the two dim neon circles that framed the clock.
  I viewed this clock as being the most important in the world.
  All other clocks were hideous and false.
Gail wore nylons. I would put my hand up her dress
  and it would stay there for hours. My hand would move about slowly,
  cautiously, always on the brink, like a young bird in a nest
high in a pine tree. The hands of the clock never moved.
  They never moved because I would not allow them to move.
  But, then they did move, and we drifted apart like two leaves
falling deep in the woods.

THE OLD HEART

With age the old heart
becomes more unlikely
to fall in love.

After all the many loves
it might become hardened
or

it becomes so obviously lazy
and fat
like a toad sitting on a couch,

left there by a
child who has been told
numberless times before

not to bring toads
into the house.
So, yes,

that is what the old heart
is like.
It has grown fat and slimy

and it doesn't move and it
should be
thrown out

the back door.

AUGUST

I go out to the shed with my father since he is having problems
with his mower, something I know nothing about. Once inside
he bends over the machine and repeatedly tries to start it, but
nothing happens. It coughs, burps, and then just goes silent.
He stands there, also silent, staring at the floor until finally
he looks at me and apologizes for not having the slightest
idea of what to do. This, from a man who at one time could
take an engine apart and put it back together blindfolded.
We close the shed and walk back to the house.
It's August. The leaves are black. The sky is white with
blue clouds. He wants to die in his sleep or by sitting
in the car with the engine running in a closed garage.
At the side of the bed every night he prays with his
rosary beads for the salvation of others. He does not
believe in time anymore. Time is nothing but a pack
of lies that stinks from urine. He asks me how old I am
and, when I tell him, his feet stop moving and he gawks
at me, dumfounded. After washing up in the garage,
the first thing he does when we get in the house is to
tell my mother how old I am, expecting her to be
equally astonished. But she ignores him, continuing
to watch a cooking show. There's a tiny woman on,
whose hands do not appear connected to her body.
She is standing below a tree full with cherry blossoms.
She is preparing a very exotic dish of grilled shrimp.
My father asks me if I have a girlfriend. He advises me
to shave off my gray beard and that I should not
grow old alone. If I don't have a girlfriend, he tells me that
I should pray for one.

READING MARQUEZ

I find it is a good time in my life to be reading the autobiography
of Gabriel Garcia Marquez. When Marquez was a child he was
able to gain the attention of adults by telling stories in which he
greatly distorted the details. As an adult he carried this
lovely habit into the writing of his books, even when it came time
to tell the story of his life. The beautiful, magical occurrences that
take place in this telling make it easier for me to accept the horrors
of Alzheimer's that plague my father. His twisted, misshapen
memories, his hallucinations, his forgetting from one moment
to the next, his face contorting with fear; all this seems slightly more
bearable to me when I feel like a fish at the bottom of the sea
looking up at the stars crying in their infancy. Unfortunately,
Marquez is of no help whatsoever to my mother. His disease
might be the death of her before it is the death
of him. The amount of patience needed to interact with my father
is almost too much to ask of a person. Yesterday
she ended up in the bank crying to a teller. Crying
in public is becoming more and more frequent for her.
She doesn't know from one day to the next what awaits her.
It's questionable whether we will have a birthday party
for him this summer. Would he be able to play the role
of a birthday person with even a stitch of understanding
and joyfulness? Would he recognize who came to the party to
celebrate his being ninety years old? Would everyone
appear as a dangerous stranger? Would the gathering
cause him to be capsized in dark bewilderment and sorrow? But,
he has always said that he wanted to live to be one hundred.
Now this miraculous event might indeed come to pass, at
least in his head, since when he last spoke of the subject he
proclaimed that he will be one hundred on his next birthday. And
if he recognizes not a soul at the party, then it will no doubt
feel to him as though he has lived "a hundred years of solitude."

BREAKFAST WITH THE SHEEP

On my way back from the bakery, where I picked up a coffee and hard roll,
I take the long way home. When I come to an open field I park the car and
decide to have my small breakfast with the sheep. About the sheep,

it's obvious their fleece was shorn recently. In the cold morning air
they gather around the one large tree that is close to the barn.
They look so skinny and vulnerable, and as though shivering.

But it is spring and just because I'd be shivering under that tree, if
I were standing there nude, that doesn't mean a sheep would be.
Any sheep in good health should be able to stay warm. Perhaps

some old sheep in a weakened state would be shivering. But, what do
I know about sheep? Nothing. I can only stare at them out of curiosity.
And they stare back at me, at least the young ones do. Apparently

the older ones can't be bothered. No doubt the older ones took one look
at me and knew I was harmless. They know I am alone, living alone, that
I am lonely. They can tell by looking into my eyes, even at this distance,

that I am one of them. Perhaps they can detect that I am a poet, and
they know down deep in their sensitive bones that poets are just as dumb
and just as helpless as sheep. Why are poets dumb as sheep? Certainly not

because we could be led off to the slaughterhouse as quietly as sheep.
We would go kicking and screaming like pigs. Myself, I need more time
to write that one poem that will bring at least a modicum of comfort

to some other dumb animal in this petty world. I am embarrassed to say
that this is all that I might prove to be good for. But, in all likelihood, my
great accomplishment will be my ability to gaze up, in my dumb silence,

at a starry night and understand that in that moment I am doing so for
the very first and the very last time.
I like having breakfast with the sheep, and if I am not looking at the sheep,

then I am looking above them for that omen-bearing cloud that will let me
know exactly when I will again have a woman in my life.
The last woman. The one who will stand naked with me under the tree

as we embrace in dumb silence, both of us shivering a little bit less.

ANDREAS

For bookmarks, I like to use postcards.
In the book I'm currently reading I'm
using a postcard of a painting by da Vinci.

It shows three of the apostles,
Bartholomaeus, Jacobus and
Andreas, at the last supper.

I imagine there must be
other postcards of this painting
depicting the rest of the apostles.

In this one, Bartholomaeus and Jacobus
seem bent on gaining the attention of Andreas.
As if wanting to avoid them

Andreas is looking the other way. In fact,
he is gesturing with his hands
as though to say that it is not necessary

that he be reminded of an agreement
they have only recently embarked upon.
Or perhaps he simply wishes not to be

reminded that any supper with Jesus
could be the last supper, knowing
just how shaky the situation has become.

It might seem that, being the highly
sociable fellow that he is, Andreas cannot
bear to think that they should discontinue

enjoying one another's company. And
since it is deeply believed that Jesus is
their divine light and guidance, then surely

Jesus will take it upon himself, given the chance,
to attend any upcoming suppers. His presence
will ensure that these suppers will be blessed

with an abundance of loaves and fishes and
there will be plenty of wine to go around.
And even if Jesus should again start turning

bread and wine into his own body and blood,
Andreas knows he will be able to ignore this
for the sake of a good time. After all, it is

not like Jesus to purposely cause a commotion;
he simply gets carried away with himself at times.
The only real problem Andreas perceives is in

the person of Judas (who, like Jesus, is not even
on the postcard). Judas, true to his nature,
is drinking heavily again. Instead of

letting everyone enjoy their meals in peace
and harmony, he has been telling dirty jokes,
boasting sexual exploits, trying to borrow money

and, worst of all, backbiting poor Jesus. However,
this does not prove to be an annoyance to Andreas.
In the past week or so, he, Bartholomaeus and

Jacobus have been devising a plan to
permanently rid Judas from their group.
The next time Judas gets thoroughly drunk,

when he is on one of his more obnoxious sprees,
they will lure him into a boat and they will
row out to the sea's deep. Once

there, innocently adrift, they will
make him a very substantial wager
that he, Judas, cannot walk on water.

A MORNING IN APRIL

I meet my mother at the lawyer's office in town.
We thought it best to talk about my being given
health care proxy and power of attorney for
my father without him initially being present.
The lawyer's on Main Street. He has new shoes.
He is a very quiet and accommodating man with overly
bushy eyebrows that might crawl off
his forehead at any second. His secretary, the older one,
performs all the small talk about the weather.
The younger is obsessed with eating a bowl of frosted flakes.
We are in there for a very long half an hour,
charged one hundred dollars which I find cheap. Afterwards,
I suggest to my mother that we have coffee together,
but she says she should get back to the house as soon
as possible since my father is being looked after by a neighbor.
So, crossing the street, I walk her to her car. She holds
onto my hand. Her hand is the hand of a woman in her eighties.
It is diminished and bony but still capable of being firm.
She was an exceptionally beautiful woman. Still is. I was always
so proud of the fact, when I was a kid, of just how beautiful
my mother was. Naturally enough, I could never understand how
my father had managed to actually have this woman in his life.
I lived with the suspicions that he could read such thoughts in
my eyes. But, I'm well aware of the fact that their love endures
on a level I may never know. I feel like weeping right here
in the street. I help her into her car. She makes a u-turn and
drives off in the direction rain is coming from. I stand there,
rooted in front of a closed movie theater in a decaying town
that lies between a river and a creek. It is a morning in April.
At some point Alzheimer's could force us to put my father in
a nursing home. I don't talk to my mother about this too much.
We know the possibility exists. I dread the day when
I'll be responsible for separating them. It will be like
tearing the wings off a bird and throwing them up in the air and
expecting them to fly.

WATCHING SPARROWS

The sparrows that come to the garden are gray.
They are the gray of the long beards of old men

who long ago managed to wear out their welcome.
They are the gray of the sorrowful eyes of women

who mourn the loss of children in wars that are so many.
But it is not easy to watch sparrows in such a heavy mist.

These birds peck at flat slabs of stone to thrive on
food that is invisible. They appear loosely constructed

out of ash, as though a sudden breeze could destroy them.
I let the curtain drop. Perhaps my staring at them might also

destroy them.

POETRY HAS RUINED ME

My father likes to tell people that poetry has ruined my life.
He has said this so often that it doesn't bother me anymore.

All my life he has been a source of negative comment.
And as far as poetry goes, whether it has ruined my life

or not, well, there is some truth to the fact that it has done
exactly that. For example, because of poetry I will never

keep a lawn neatly cut. All my lawns will grow wild and
the weeds will have their way. Whatever car I own will be

a jalopy. It will be ancient and it will be rusty and the insides
will always be piled up with newspapers and model airplanes

(if I ever attempt building and flying such things). My house
will be in shambles, eaten to the ground by poetry as though

by crazed termites. My ruined life will have ruined children
in it. They, in turn, will have ruined children of their own

who will go out and ruin the four corners of the world.
My wife will be ruined. I will ruin her with poetry just as

I have ruined my life. In time her hair will turn white and
her teeth will turn black. Her skin will rot with ruin.

All this will happen because I write poetry. I will die
from writing poetry. I will be ruined in my grave,

honored in heaven.

TEMPORARILY A TURN FOR THE BETTER

When I call my mother on a Sunday morning,
usually we find ourselves indulging in a lot
of small talk having to do with family matters.
Today, however, the conversation took on a
rather serious tone, since it focused in on my
father's senility and how it seems to be affecting
his personality. So far, there is agreement
on the fact that his personality has taken a turn
for the better, that he is much easier to be with,
that his anger and depression have lessened.
My mother says he is also quite a bit more loving,
more thoughtful and considerate in ways he
never was before. Any morning now, she says,
she would not be shocked to see him in the yard
feeding birds. The birds, landing on his shoulders
and outstretched arms, singing their little hearts out,
bellies stuffed with seeds and bread, stuffed with
my father's favorite homemade black raspberry jam.

THE LINE IN THE WATER

I return to the house late in the afternoon.
I walk through the front door, then out the
back door and continue through thick grass.

I make my way up to the acorn-yellow barn
where the old landlord lives in the summertime.
We'll indulge in small talk and perhaps make

plans to do something together later on. Today
a note tacked to the barn door informs me that
he is at the pond. I find him sitting in a lawn chair,

reading a book of short stories by Chekhov.
A fishing pole is on the ground next to him,
the line in the water. He tells me to look in a

plastic bag that is on the dock, at the two trout
he has caught (at the beginning of every summer
he has the pond stocked). At the sight of them

I feel a brief slippery rush of anticipation, since
I know he'll give me one and I love pan frying trout.
But I also feel a sadness over losing these two fish.

I had found joy in simply watching them break
the surface of the water when feeding on insects.
Then a sticky breeze of anxiety sweeps over me.

I wonder if he had hooked the golden carp by accident.
He assures me that that had not happened, that
the carp is not tempted by anything on a hook.

The carp and I are connected. I had saved its life when
it was trapped in a creek after heavy flooding receded.
It is anyone's guess how it had become trapped there.

I had taken the carp from the creek with net and bucket;
transferred it to the pond where it very quickly felt at home.
It shows no fear of humans. Whenever I arrive at the pond

it swims over to me, no doubt looking for something to eat.
I'm told I should feed it corn. I worry that
another heavy rainstorm will wash it from this pond, and

it will again get stuck in the creek, eventually
to perish there. But there's nothing I can do to prevent this
from happening. For that matter, I see myself in

the near future being washed away, in the sense that
I'll be moving on after living here for close to twenty years.
The forces of change will simply wash me away.

When I came to live here I was a young man; when I leave
I will be an old one. I came to live here with a
beautiful woman; when I leave, as it stands now, I will leave

alone. And like the carp, eventually I'll get stuck
downcreek somewhere, and I'll perish when the creek goes
through a drying out period. I settle into a chair

next to the old landlord and we look out over the placid water,
made all the more placid by the removal of the trout.
They feed no more, their dreamy presence no more made known

by the snatching of insects off the surface of the water.
When I mention this, the landlord's indifference is expressed by a
soft philosophical shrug of the shoulders. He prefers

talking about the Chekhov he has read, about the misery
of the peasants, the boredom of the land-owning gentry
at the turn of the century. It's early August. The sky is overcast.

Thunder can be heard coming from distant battlefields
where blades of grass refuse to be influenced by blood.
A fishing pole is on the ground next to the landlord,

the line in the water.

THE FOOL

(after a Zen legend)

I ride backwards on an ox
I ride through the center of town

I am without the people's concerns
They gawk at me and laugh at me

and pronounce me the fool
They beat me and steal my ox

They slaughter it and
in a cloud of flies they feast on it

I crawl home to stare in the dark
The screaming of the ox impossible

to rid from my ears.

TWO WEEKS AGO

I see my father sitting in his rocker in the solar room
and so I hand him the paper. My mother is busy cooking
so I set the table, and it is while I am doing this that I notice
my father staring at a picture on the front page of Jesus Christ
wearing a crown of thorns that are making his head bleed.
He keeps staring at this picture like a mouse staring at poison.
So I step out into the solar room and ask him how he is doing.
He looks up from his rocker with a weary sadness in his eyes.
He looks back at the paper and points to the picture and says
that what they did to this fellow is a crying shame. I tell him
that it is only a picture from a movie that has just come out.
My father says, "Oh no no no," and pressing a finger firmly
into the chest of Jesus Christ he informs me that this event
happened only two weeks ago, in New Jersey.

TO DISTRACTION

Why must you lie in bed like that, on your stomach
with just blouse and panties on, propped up on elbows,
reading that vegetarian cookbook you picked up in

the health food store? Why don't you put some clothes on
and go sit on the porch, where there is a wonderful breeze
this fine afternoon in late June? And where did you

dig up those skimpy panties from? I swear, never have I seen
them before. I have all of your underclothes memorized.
They must be new ones, or could it be I've just never noticed

them before because there isn't much of them to notice,
although I hardly think this could be the case. And why
in hell is your skin so incredibly white? It's

a simple question. I am not nagging you. When was the
last time you ventured out into the sunlight? You know
the sheer untouched whiteness of your skin drives me

to distraction. Look at me, standing helpless in the doorway.
I am riveted to the spot. I am mesmerized by the
unbelievable roundness of your ass. My eyes want to

roll over this roundness like I used to roll my toy cars and
trucks over my mother's body in bed, when I would find her
sleeping after my father had gone off early to work.

I want to inhale the roundness of your ass as I would inhale
a ripe pumpkin split open in autumn. I want to spit
wet watermelon pits on the roundness of your ass and

watch them stick there, so that I can pick them off with
my wet trembling lips to swallow them whole. Tell me,
how am I supposed to go out and water the young flowers

when you are occupying the bed this way? If we were
at the beach you would be asking me to spray your
long legs with water. Other men stare at me with envy

in their hearts. It's true, I've seen this happen. Often
I wonder how such a beautiful woman has fallen in love
with me. There is no answer, other than dumb luck.

Or if your love for me is simply an expression of life
being kind to me, then I can only hope that death
be at least half so kind.

MOODY OLD ME

Moody old me
boring the pants
off myself

wasting the hours
of the day and
making the night dull

Moody old me
driving down the road
slow as a horse and buggy

talking to myself or
just repeating the blues
heard on the radio

Moody old me
washing dishes in the dark
and one wine glass too

thinking of tomorrow
waking up at dawn
lonely as a prayer

Moody old me
buying bread
cheap and white

living with a
jelly stain on the couch
from when she lived here

centuries ago.

STILL ALIVE

During the war my father wanted to join the navy
to serve on a submarine but failed the physical, the
reason being that his top teeth did not come down
in front of his bottom teeth. They came down
directly on top of them. What this had to do with
life in a submarine he was never able to fully explain, but
every time he told this story, never did he fail to demonstrate how
exactly his teeth were afflicted with what you might think as being
one awfully small and insignificant disability. Not allowed
to join the navy, he remained with his factory job. Discontent
with this, though, and wanting to satisfy his patriotic spirit, he
then decided to join the army. On his way down to recruiting
he encountered a soldier at the bus stop, who was waiting for the
same bus my father was waiting for. Maybe looking to make
a little conversation, my father asked the soldier what it was like
to be in the army. The soldier, so the story goes, looked at
my father as though he were joking or simply daft. He said
that if you wanted to spend your life digging ditches then the army
was the perfect place to be. Possessing zero desire to dig even
one ditch, my father never joined the army. For the remainder
of his days the closest he ever came to experiencing combat was
when he would watch war movies on TV. Throughout
my childhood he never indulged in any after dinner conversation,
or, as far as that goes, not even that much during dinner. After
he was finished mopping up his plate with buttered bread he would,
without fail, disappear into the parlor. Many a night there would be
a war movie on loud and you'd hear the sound of gunfire and
bombs dropping, soldiers screaming in agony. For those of us who
remained at the table it felt as though dessert was being eaten
at the front, as though the apple pie and ice cream would be best
consumed in a fox hole. Whenever a commercial would come on
he'd come strolling back into the kitchen, maybe for more dessert.
I'd always be amazed that he was still alive.

SERMON TO THE BIRDS

A little painting hangs over the headboard
  of my bed, about the size of one of those trays
  a waiter brings to your table with the check on it.
The scene depicts Saint Francis of Assisi giving a
  sermon to birds. He thought of them as being his
  brothers and his sisters. They appear
trusting and unafraid, and in their midst
  Saint Francis is holding his arms open as though
  offering them his blessing. Another man
in the painting is wearing similar monk clothing
  but is without a halo. The lack of a halo bespeaks
  of a man not in possession of an equal amount of holiness.
If he were alone, no doubt the birds would scatter in fear. Years ago
  this reproduction was given to me by a painter. He would
  sell his work for a pittance to support his wanderings.
Recently when paging through a book in the library
  I came across the original. It made me think back
  to when I was young and starting out all over again.
I had met this painter when I was working at a motel
  for about five years, right after my divorce.
  He was well over six feet tall, had long red hair,
full beard and dazzling blue eyes. One morning
  he needed to get to a neighboring town west of the motel.
  I had nothing better to do, so I gave him a lift.
It was when we were parting that he gave me
  the painting of Saint Francis giving a sermon to the birds.
  On the back of it he had signed his name under
a few words of thanks. The painting has always been
  dear to me, perhaps because it was done by a painter
  who so freely roamed the earth. He had the smile of
a simple man. He had made a simple living and was
  the happiest of painters. I remember
  shivering with envy whenever
  I was in his presence.

THE SHEEP

Since she started living here,
 there is this charcoal drawing of two sheep
  hanging in the bedroom. I think
  when I asked her about it she said
  she had purchased it some years back
 at an auction. It's on the wall facing
  the foot of the bed. Often, when
  lying in bed daydreaming, I'll stare at those sheep
as though I am waiting for them to move.
  It does not appear to be a finished drawing,
  rather just an exercise in drawing animals.
Some parts of the sheep show a concentration
  of heavy line work, especially the faces
  and the feet. I can't say that I would have
purchased this drawing myself, although,
  in all truth, I have never bid on anything at auction.
  God only knows what
I would have come away with if I had.
  It is an evening light that falls on
  the sheep now, a winter evening light, a light
not much good for doing anything.
  The sheep's faces look black and I cannot
  make out their features. There are only
two of them, and they appear
  standing perfectly still. They would be
  no help in putting me to sleep. I can't
imagine them even jumping over a snake.
  Yet my eyes are heavy, and I should nap
  until the woman who owns these sheep returns.
I like these sheep, precisely
  because they are doing nothing. They are
  gloriously dumb animals.
Periodically they will emit
                sounds of pain.

A GOOD SIGN

In the morning she comes into the office
 at the motel and hands me the book of
  Chinese poems she borrowed nearly a year ago.
 I'm genuinely happy to see her and I throw
my arms around her, and when I do I think she
displays about the same amount of happiness
 when she throws her arms around me.
Where this happiness has come from is as much
a mystery to her as it is to me, I'm sure, considering
 we've only spent a single night together, and
 that was about a year ago when I had lent her
the book of Chinese poems. I'm not on duty,
 so we go for a walk on the outskirts of town.
It's a blowy autumn day, and we are both
bundled in sweaters. Conversation is erratic,
 sometimes approaching the awkward side, but
 by some precious small miracle it manages to
purr along nicely enough. When I look at her,
 I cannot help but think of the recent women
 in my life, the miniature uncaring affairs, and
I wonder whether we could ever have anything better.
 Perhaps she is wondering this very same question.
 I cannot tell. How many men have I seen her
around town with? But this I cannot dwell on.
 Our stroll takes us into the woods where
 we come upon a long log, which, because of rot,
is very soft, very comfortable to sit on.
 I tell her that her lips look very nourished.
 But that's as far as it goes. And after awhile
I have to go behind a tree to take a piss.
 As I stand there in the cold shadows
 I think about just how chilly it is, about the
book of Chinese poems that I have in
 my possession again; and I try to figure out
 my bearings with this woman, struggling for
some clue that might tip me off as to the direction
 we might be going in. When I turn to see
 how she is doing, I see her squatting
in the leaves, also taking a piss.
 This I take as being a good sign.

UPON THE RIVER

I cannot remember the sound of rain or bird.
I cannot remember the sound of train or boat.
I do not want to remember the sound of the black river.
Although I do remember the green fish that could be seen.
I wondered how they were able to survive in such water.
The snow was a different story. It seemed beautiful and pure
and it would bring all of life to an enchanted standstill.
There were bridges and tunnels and a tall city in the distance.
There was a mountain ash tree at one of my bedroom windows.
No philosophers or saints or poets dared live in our town.
There was a man who sharpened blades in his cellar and
a woman whose nose turned red from the perfume of other women.
On summer nights there were lots of large iridescent beetles.
On autumn nights there were lots of large yellow leaves.
On winter nights there were lots of large snowy moons.
On spring nights mothers put infants in baskets and
set them adrift upon the river of mysterious green fish.

ANOTHER DAY

Blue Jay screaming
at my bedroom window
reminds me of my father

the father of my childhood
the way he'd yell at me
on a Saturday morning

that I should get out of bed
that I had two good healthy arms
and two good healthy legs and

that I didn't know how lucky I was
that children in China had neither
arms nor legs so I should get up

out of the damned bed and
I should go out and weed the lawn
do something

anything
anything that might indicate I was
worthy of being fed another day.

MY FIRST JOB

The house on River Road, where I started living at the age of five,
was located right across from the little league field.
Night games were played under the lights. It was a beautiful sight,
that field so brilliant on a warm summer evening with
the black Passaic River right there in the background.
Our neighbor, Howard, an old navy man, would sit out
on his patio smoking his pipe, watching those games.
Without fail he would stand very erect and very proper
when the national anthem was played. When cutting his lawn, with
o such meticulous care, he'd walk as though marching
on parade. My father, to make extra money after dinner,
repaired lawnmowers in the basement.
He and Howard loved talking about mowers and lawn care.
Sometimes my father would sit out on the patio with
Howard, watching the cars going by on that busy,
narrow road, the mosquito truck occasionally among them.
They'd watch the ballgame, sure, but my father had
no real love for the game and, in fact, he did everything to
discourage my playing it. I never did join a team. Instead,
he arranged for me to have a job sweeping up garbage after
each game. This he recognized as being a worthwhile
occupation for a young boy. I was getting paid at the end of
each week, whereas the ballplayers were making nothing.
My father believed that money was the most important thing
in life. Since they would stick to the asphalt under the stands,
Popsicle wrappers were
the hardest to sweep up.

ROVER

Stickball we played at the far end of the stadium.
We'd draw a chalk strike zone on the wall there.
Touch football we played in the street. None
of the kids I hung around with played organized ball.
We'd stay outside until dark, or until one of us was called in.
In the dark seasons, often it'd get to the point where
the ball was almost impossible to see sailing through the air.
When it was dinnertime, my father would whistle for me. This,
of course, was cause for undying ridicule from the other kids.
They'd start barking like dogs and calling me Rover.
I would be sitting at the table minding my own business
and I'd hear them mercilessly raising fun at my expense.
My father never made the connection between his whistling and
all the barking going on outside. He'd sit at the head of the table
drinking shots of whiskey, buttering bread and vehemently
complaining about people. And I'd sit there, silent as grass,
deathly afraid of spilling even one drop of his precious milk.

THE DEAD BIRD

Reading about Albert Pinkham Ryder
 (in an essay by Updike) I came across
  the painting called The Dead Bird,
  completed on the top of a cigar box.
I was intrigued by the painting, but
  even more so by the name of the painting.
 I was reminded of the dead bird (a heron,
to be precise) which I had found in
  the stream out back. This happened
 a few days ago and since then I've been
trying to write a five-line poem about
  this bird, but without any success. And now,
  after looking at Ryder's painting, the idea of
this poem has taken on increased importance.
  I figure that if I put the poem in a manuscript
 I could then call the manuscript, "The Dead Bird."
Grim, I admit, but I know if I were
  to come across a book with this title
 I would not have the strength to refrain from
picking it up. Harmless as it may seem,
  the encounter with a dead bird
(in the title of a book) is rife with bad omen (so
my dear sweet mother has
  been telling me since early childhood)
  and to choose to ignore it invites tragedy.
In the case of the heron, I attempted
  to counteract any such omen by dumping
 the ashes of a notebook of poems on the bird.
(Okay, I sound like a superstitious dunce
  living alone in the woods now for too long).
 I had been able to salvage nothing of any value
from this notebook, so, without regret
  had thrown its entire contents into the woodstove.
 When I then took and dumped these ashes
on the dead bird, the cloud
  that rose up from them cheered me immeasurably.
 It looked as though the spirit of the bird
had been released into the cold autumn air.
  Or, it was simply a cloud of poems, poems
 that had, in the end, served a good purpose.
The omen had been nullified and for one brief
  and trembling moment these otherwise worthless
  poems had served a good and sublime purpose.

GREAT CATCHES

Because my head was underneath the couch,
I was taking punches directly in my rib cage.
My father had just gotten home from work and
we had argued, and before I knew what happened
we were embroiled in a fist fight. I was in my
second year of high school and had been thrown off
the track team for behaving like a deranged juvenile.
The Christian Brothers didn't know how to deal with me,
other than slapping me silly or simply banishing me
from sight. Between the beatings I absorbed from
the brothers, the nuns and my father, youth was a time
riddled with fear. When I was in 7th grade a very old, very
insane nun found a love poem I had written to my girlfriend.
This earned me a trip to the stationery room where she
unleashed the most miraculously hellish whipping using
a long green stick, the kind flowers are attached to
in order to place them in the ground at a gravesite.
Her strength was damned remarkable. She had me
prancing around in a circle like a regular circus pony. Perhaps
I had reminded her of a lover in her youth, one who had
jilted her, squashing her heart like a tomato, sending her
fleeing to the sanctuary of a nunnery where only the love
of Jesus could make her heart whole and trusting again.
What had freed me from my father's punches, that day
I was trapped underneath the couch, was my mother
dragging my father off of me and allowing me to escape.
But he followed me and hunted me down in my bedroom
where he resumed his attack, again causing my mother to
rescue me by jumping between us. When he wouldn't back off
she slapped him so hard that he was reduced to a mound
of stunned flesh. From this mound his eyes glared, not a
threatening glare, rather it was the shocked glare of a fish
that has just realized that the whole lake has been drained
of water. At that moment I wanted nothing more than to
embrace and hold him and offer what comfort I could.
He was alone and vulnerable in a cold and terrible world.
But before I could do anything of the kind, he left the room
with my mother in close pursuit, my bedroom suddenly
reduced to feeling like a tree having lost every leaf in a storm.
What could I do but grab my baseball mitt from the clothes tree, sit
down on the edge of the bed and bury my face in the pocket
and inhale, deeply, all the great catches no one had ever
seen me make.

THE WALKING STICK AND THE HAIKU

Drinking water at the window above the kitchen sink,
I watch my father working in his garden and I notice
how much he is starting to resemble a walking stick.
Not a stick a person would walk with, but the insect that
looks like a stick. I suppose he looks this way from
being a vegetarian and working in the garden ten hours a day.
It's about the size of a basketball court, the garden,
and there are more worms in it than there are in China. Old age,
too, is doing its best to take him down to the bone.
In the hothouse, plants just starting to make their
way into the world surround us. My father tells me
the garden this year will have twenty-three different
kinds of vegetables. We sit on stools in his hothouse,
and behind him I can see a blackboard with reminders
written in chalk. He asks me about my job and I say
the minimum, not wanting to burden him with how weary
I am of working. His skin is baked a dirty gold,
and I can't help staring at his rough hands, the veins like
swollen rivers testing the resolve of their banks.
What will happen to his garden if someday it falls into my
hands? It wouldn't last long. Only a haiku would
be left on the blackboard. Something by Issa. Something
about flies saying prayers.

I FIND AN OLD TENNIS BALL

I find an old tennis ball in the field
between the house and the barn.
It's faded lime-green and it's wet
from rain. My first inclination is

to simply chuck it in the woods.
Not wanting to confuse the trees,
I put it in a bird cage that's in the garage.
That cage has been out there

since the canary died of old age.
I figure that by putting the ball in
the cage, it will then have no chance
of rolling under my feet and tripping me

whenever I'm in the garage doing
whatever it is I do when I'm out there.
Also, in this way, the bird cage is
once again put to good use, instead

of just standing there empty and
without song. Well, it will still be
without song, true. A tennis ball
cannot sing, as everyone well knows.

Even if I cut a hole in it and squeezed it
there would be only a faint rush of air.
Although if I were to repeatedly squeeze it
I bet it would almost sound as though

it were breathing. In a sense,
I'd be bringing a life to this ball that
it has never known before, not even
when flying back and forth over the net

on the clearest of sunny days.
But perhaps it was a ball
purchased only to be given
to a dog to play with. After all,

the world is filled with objects
made for one purpose then used
for another. One obvious example
is the bed. It was made for people

to sleep in, but how many people
use it also to weep in. This
is not to say that when a woman
weeps in her bed (perhaps because

she has been abandoned by her lover)
she is then concerned with the fact
that she is misusing the bed.
At that moment she is consumed

by loss and sorrow
and the bed is simply
the most sensible place in her life
to retreat to. At one point

she will bury her face in the pillow
and it will soak up her tears.
Now, pillows are not made with
the idea in mind of soaking up tears,

but who can argue that they aren't
perfectly suited for such a task.
And I would like to point out the
exotic Chilean white-breasted sparrow,

that makes its nest in city trees,
utilizing paper from cigarette butts
found near the tables of sidewalk cafes.
Now tell me, what god would create

such a beautiful little bird to clean up
after a bunch of people smoking and
drinking in an attempt to find refuge
from the unending miseries of this world?

And what man or woman would roll a cigarette
with the intention that
its remains be used
for the nest of a bird?

TO BE AFRAID OF FIRE AGAIN

For awhile I didn't believe in anything.
I didn't believe in birth, death, the gods.
I didn't believe in eating, drinking, sleeping.
I didn't even believe in making love anymore.
Luckily I didn't stay this way for long.
Soon I was afraid of fire again. I cleaned
every crumb out of the toaster. And it felt good
to be afraid of fire again. I wanted to play with it.

LIVING IN SIN

My father repeatedly tells the same stories, whereas,
with age, my mother does just the opposite.
She'll tell stories about her childhood no one
has ever heard before. I don't know if she's doing this
to emphasize how differently they are aging,
or whether these stories simply come to mind.
As for my father, it's hard to determine whether he even
listens to what she is saying. His is a world I fear.
The other night he woke before dawn, put his
best suit on, woke my mother and proclaimed that
it was about time they finally tied the knot.
This, after being married for over sixty years.
This, from a man who swears that in all his life
he has never broken even one of the Ten Commandments.

CEMETERY COUNTRY

When I was 4 I was given a Hopalong Cassidy outfit which, I'm told,
I insisted on wearing every day for the entire summer.
That was the last year we lived on Rutherford Place, in one
of the apartment buildings that had a row of garages out back.
Behind the garages was a huge cemetery, which had no trouble
taking up most of the town. Often my mother would remind me
that it was in this cemetery that she first walked me in a carriage.
As an infant I attended more burials than most people attend
in a lifetime. She said she'd simply blend us into the crowds and
no one would notice us and be suspicious.
This cemetery was my first playground. Sometimes
my friend, Cookie, who dressed like a doll, would join me
on my exploits. She was older (not by much), had a head of
unruly blonde curls and she walked as though her spine was made
out of a willow branch. Whatever we ended up doing, she was
always on the lookout for an insect in need of medical attention.
In her cellar she ran a hospital for insects. But in all
the time I knew her, I remember her finding only one insect which
she thought she could save. It was a bee. She had taken it back
to her hospital and had placed it in a small matchbox. It
almost looked like a coffin. And, sure enough, the next morning
the bee was dead. After that her cellar felt more like a morgue.
So yes, at an early age I was well aware of death. From
the kitchen window, on the third floor, I had watched burials.
I could see beyond the cemetery to the buildings of Manhattan.
But, in my child's mind, I thought that these building were
situated at the far end of the cemetery. I didn't even know
they were buildings, rather I thought that they were the
largest gravestones. For me, the future was a time when
I would finally be brave enough to venture out to those
faraway gravestones, when I'd finally be able to read
the words carved into them.

THERE IS THERE

So, while my mother is getting dinner ready
I ask my father about the cars he has owned.
I ask him if he remembers his first car.
He simply shrugs. Having owned so many cars
he has no idea which one was the first one.
My mother chimes in, saying that the first car
she remembers my father owning was the one
he had on the night they met, the one in which
she had given him a firm slap across the face
when he had placed his hand on her knee.
She says it was a black coupe. This car doesn't
seem to ring a bell for my father, but he seems
suddenly able to remember the Hudson which
they had owned right after I was born. It was a
sleek, long gray haunted looking thing
which my father speaks of with great fondness.
This car seems to help him to remember others.
As he muses over them he asks me why I'm asking,
and I tell him that I intend to write a poem about
these cars. At this sweet morsel of sad information
he simply wags his head in wonderment and disbelief.
But I keep writing down the facts as my mother takes
a fish out of the fridge, unfolds the white paper
and sticks her finger exactly where you might imagine
the heart was once located. I hear her
saying something about the Hudson eventually
having been sold to her sister Judy's husband, a man
named Zeke. My father asks who this Zeke person is
and we remind him. Then, just as my mother
is putting the fish in the oven, my father proudly
lets it be known that through all the years of driving
he never once had a flat tire and that, since
he is no longer allowed to drive, undoubtedly he will
live the rest of his life without ever experiencing one.
He estimates living at most maybe another two years,
appearing relieved to be so close to the end. That said,
he reminds my mother not to forget to make tartar sauce.
She says that it's already on the table, right in front of him.
Stunned, he asks," Where?" And she says, "Right there."
And he asks, "Where is there?" And she says, "There is there."
And he says, "That's your opinion."

A POET

It is a good night for pissing outside.
The moon is full and it is showering
  an orange light over the back field.
The katydids are gone, or at least quiet
for reasons I'm unaware of. The only sound
is a cricket, which must be poor at letting go
  of what is already lost. Autumn
  has been making some very serious inroads.
If I walk through the field, far enough, I can see
  the moon drifting over cold pines on
the other side of the road, where a mailbox stands
empty as an unneeded and forgotten shoebox.
  Slamming the back door, I frighten deer away
  from underneath the apple tree, where
the pickings are especially rich.
  A bit drunk, I let out a feeble call,
  desperate, almost, to remind the deer
that I am absolutely harmless. It's doubtful
  they don't hear me. I just wonder
  if they believe me. Perhaps they don't trust me,
and that thought, that possibility,
  for a poet,
  is scary.

WEARY

My father shows me around the cellar as though
he's a real estate agent and I'm a potential buyer.
There's a beautiful yet horrifying
innocence to the early stages of Alzheimer's. When
we return to the small island in the kitchen for dessert,
he starts questioning us, wondering why all the visitors,
who were never here, have departed. What
can my mother and I do but exchange knowing glances?
When I'm leaving she walks me out to my car.
She's eighty-three, weary, scared and not sleeping nights.
Any slightest sound wakes her. She's lost twenty pounds.
Behind her, in the solar room, I see my father holding up
one of the cats. It hangs limp in his large hands.
it looks like a stuffed animal he has forgotten how to wind.

SHE LOVED MOZART

There's a sadness to it, of course, my becoming more
   and more isolated from the world. I remember, years ago,
    when I was living at the motel, there was this woman who
    used to come and go, sometimes staying for months at a time.
   Every so often I'd go over to her room, sit around, and talk with her.
The room would smell from clove cigarettes and dirty wash.
   Over the lampshades pieces of clothing were draped, to bring
   the light down to the most remarkable dimness. This light
never failed to charm and attract me, as a moth would be
   attracted to a bright light (although, I suppose moths are
   drawn to dim light also). Anyway, I find myself steadily
becoming increasingly like this woman, and it's not always
   the most comfortable realization. Although, I cannot say
   that I am living with dirty wash. No, this I cannot admit to.
If anything, I'm fanatical about washing clothes. My
   clothing has worn thin, not from my wearing it but from
   the continuous washings. But, my god, like this woman
I'm letting the house go dark. She died at the motel, from cancer.
   Some nights I'd see her crossing the parking lot, meager flesh
   on her bones, and she'd knock on my door and she'd ask me
to play Mozart on my stereo set. She loved Mozart.
   In her youth she had been a very promising violist, but
   injury and shock from a fire had made her a ghost
of her old talent, her old self. I used to feed her also,
   the miniscule amount she was capable of eating.
   She loved sharing a thin sandwich as much as
she loved Mozart. I told her it takes
   a lot of solitude to write a poem.
   She told me it takes a lot of solitude
   to die.

NEW AIR

Rain, off and on, falling through thin trees
  and their small jittery leaves. And the wind, it's
throwing the tops of the trees in every direction,
against a dark purple sky which is staging thunderstorms
  which never seem to get any closer. By dawn,
a cold front is expected to come down from Canada, and to
welcome it I'll leave the bedroom window open.
  I want the cold to greet me when I wake.
The warmth and the mugginess has almost been
too suffocating to bear. I fully expect
  the old cotton curtains upstairs to come back to life
with fresh enthusiasm and, if I'm lucky, the
new air might help rejuvenate my own
  feeble way of dealing with things.

THE PITCHFORK AND THE POEM

I pick up my father's ashes at the funeral parlor.
When I enter I hear a voice coming from the floor above,
informing me that his ashes are on the desk to the left of me,
in a box with his name on it. I take the box, put it
on the passenger seat in my car and drive off. But before
I get too far I have to pull to the side of the road, almost into
the trees, where I weep uncontrollably. Three times this happens
on the way back to my mother's house where she waits for me.
When I finally do reach her house, I put his ashes in the shed,
which was his favorite place to just sit and talk about why exactly
sitting in a dark shed, at the end of a long life, is the best place to sit.
The place is cold and the weeping exhausting. I look at his tools.
He could fix anything and was always disappointed in me, a man
who could fix nothing. Occasionally I'd help him in his garden, but
he knew I wouldn't last long, that I'd rather be in the house lounging
on the couch reading, scribbling, dozing, watching my mother cook.
When I was a kid, gardening was considered a form of punishment
and I've never been able to rid myself of this feeling; or, hell, maybe
I've been just too lazy to. And perhaps I've just been too lazy, these
many years later, to stop viewing my father as being narrow-minded
and mean-spirited. But as I sit in his shed I know
only the last years of his life: when he suffered through the memories
of being an orphan at seven; when he spoke endlessly of his deep love
for my mother; when he found solace in the realms of
pure communion with a god he could always talk to, a god who was
never unfair and who always answered his prayers. As the cold and
the darkness saturate and expose me, all I want to do is hold him,
to comfort him and myself and to weep for the passing of our lives.
There's a pitchfork in his shed, which I'll keep. He was
immensely proud of it, claiming that pitchforks are simply not made
with the same quality anymore. Poetry was useless but
a good pitchfork could help bring forth life from the earth. He never
saw equal value both in the pitchfork and the poem. I had
accepted this long ago, and eventually he had accepted that
I was a dreamer, that I had a drifter's wayward grasp of life. But
his love for me was never anything but robust and unswerving,
practically bewildering, and oftentimes, now,
I have to remind myself that whatever love I experience in life has
powerful roots in the love my parents had for me.
With my father it began the day he brought tiny red boxing gloves
dangling from a bouquet of flowers to my mother's bedside, after
she had given birth to me, a creature who would prove to be such a
lively and a mysterious source of aggravation and disappointment.
Unfailingly this love would continue, to the day I was at his bedside,
when he, demented and shriveled and dying, was still
cognizant enough to know me, to ask me if I were okay.
Somehow out of the ravages of Alzheimer's, miraculously,

it seemed this was all that mattered to him, that I was okay. Because of his love, I am aware of the stars at night looking down on me with tenderness and care, gently and brilliantly inviting me to share my dust with them and with the dust of others who have gone before me: the dust of kings, squatters, lion trainers, actors, murderers and priestesses; and the dust of a gardener, my father who loved simply sitting in his rocker in the solar room, quietly paging through seed catalogues when in winter the garden was dark and when the garden was frozen.

THE PEAR AND THE EARTH

A terrible grayness today, such a grayness
  I can barely bring myself to mention it.
   It's as though this grayness were seeping through
  the walls, filling the house as the sounds of insects
fill it at night. What is there to do but
  stand at the back door, eat a bright green pear
 and stare out at the field. While I enjoy eating the pear,
at the same time I hate to see it disappear.
  After all, it was the only effective relief from
  the otherwise overwhelming grayness. If
I'm not mistaken, I think I remember being told,
  when I was a kid in school, that the earth is not
  shaped like a ball but rather like a pear. When I consider this,
I'm sorry that I do not have the whole pear before me again,
  not only to benefit from its bright greenness but also
  that I might contemplate the true shape of the earth.
It was the last pear. There are no other pears standing
  between me and this grayness that is as persistent
  as ants or the ocean. I suppose, if the urge to muse over
the shape of the earth proves strong, I might settle for
  looking out at the field, although it's obvious that this field
  offers little to go on. And forget the idea
of there being any greenness out there. So far,
  spring has been very stingy. But I don't question this stinginess.
  It is simply how this season chooses to express itself.
For my own sanity, I must strive to be
  as generous of spirit as possible.
  I lie on the couch, holding my shaved head in my hands,
  looking at the grayness clinging to the ceiling
  like fog.

THE OLDEST SONGS

The bright sunlight against the snow
 is almost blinding, so there is no
  going outdoors without wearing sunglasses.
I sit on the front steps peeling an orange. I eat
 all the neat little sections until only the peel is left,
  and this I throw out onto the hard snow.
But the steps are much too cold to continue sitting on,
 even though the sunlight seems more intense
  than in the summer. In summer the sunlight is taken,
soaked, and darkened into green. March sunlight
 is primarily converted into a blinding atmosphere.
  The birds do not even want to fly about in it too much.
They go from branch to branch, in the same tree,
 calling out warnings to one another:
  the earth's oldest songs.

PLANTING ONIONS

Planting onions in April with my father is not such an easy chore.
We go along rows of raised earth, he on one side, I on the other.
He indicates where each seedling should be placed by poking in
the soil with a stick.   My role consists in ever so carefully
lowering the delicate plants into the holes and securely arranging
the soil around them. But no matter how careful and thoughtful
I try to be, eventually he finds fault in what I've done. His voice
starts cranking out instructions, ruthlessly, on how precisely one
should place a plant in the earth. I say nothing about his attitude,
since it wouldn't do a bit of good. I've never known him to
behave differently. He understands the roots of onions more than
he does the roots of his own bitterness. And, as far as I go, when it
comes to gardening I am uniquely clumsy and insensitive.
No doubt I'm capable of being the same with all of life.
When all the seedlings are tucked safely in the ground, he stumbles
along with hose, drenching the soil. This will cause the soil to
soak down around the roots, prohibiting the creation of air pockets.
Such pockets, he claims, will cause the roots to rot. To me,
the seedlings already look defeated. And furthermore, my god,
I wonder what all this fuss is about with regard to how I was placing
the seedlings in the ground, since according to him the watering will
correct any of the mistakes I have made, anyway. By how
he looks at the sky, with mixture of disgruntlement and relief,
I can tell evening is coming on. Shadows are spreading at the edge of
the woods. I know, from past gardens, there will be more onions than
anyone will know what to do with.

QUIET POTATOES

Another snowstorm, perhaps the largest of the many
 backbreaking ones we've already had this winter.
  Close to midnight, I step out the front door to watch
the flakes coming down, and I also get to see one of the
 mammoth plows with rotating yellow light rumbling by.
  But because I am on the brink of coming down with a cold
I don't stay out long. After making sure everything
is closed up, I climb the stairs and once in the bedroom
 I shed my outer clothing. This afternoon, in
the post office, people were talking about the hardships
 of the winter storms, but I didn't say a word. I didn't mention,
  of course, just how much I have embraced these storms:
the serenity of them, the overall sublime nature of them.
 I crawl into my bed piled with every blanket I own.
 I love the fact that the world has come to a standstill.
I find it a great blessing. I don't want to see the green yet.
 The seasons of insects and animals and returning people
  cannot hold a candle to winter's overwhelming quiet.
None of the neighbors are here during the winter months.
 The house floats in dunes of snow. Other houses
  are not visible at night because they are dark.
On the night table there is a glass of vodka.
 Vodka from Poland, made from potatoes.
  Quiet potatoes.

MY PRIZE POSSESSION

The skull of a dog hangs over the fireplace.
  On the mantelpiece there is a deck of cards,
  not used in over half a year, at least.
Nothing else hangs on the walls.
  There is almost no furniture to speak of.
  In the kitchen cabinets a few dishes reside,
along with cans of beans and a bottle containing
  the last of the olive oil I cannot afford to replace.
  In the bedroom upstairs, where I sleep, there is a futon.
In the spare bedroom on the other side of the hallway
  there is nothing but long, thin roots hanging on the wall,
that are entangled and twisting on the wall like a wreath.
I found these sacred roots in the stream, nearby
  the motel where I was living and working. To say
  that I like to keep things simple is no big revelation.
Simplicity is easy in such a large house, where ponies
  were once raised in the barn out back. The pony shoes
  I come across in the garden I hang in the woodshed.
From a great apple tree, that is in dire need of pruning,
  blossoms fall and cover the roof of this woodshed. But,
  yes, there are so many rooms, my god, certainly too many
for one person. It is rare that a visitor does not show envy.
  I moved in with a woman, but the relationship changed
  and the change left me alone and responsible for these rooms.
I cherish the skull of the dog. It is a prize possession.
  I ask it no questions, and it shows me the same courtesy.
  I'll keep it with me as I grow old. It will be the best of company.
I admire the teeth it has left.

BLACK WALNUT TREES

My father gave me some black walnut trees, two, three inches
in height. Last year, a friend of his had given him
a bag of black walnuts which he had picked from trees in
his yard. Not being able to open these nuts with ease,
my mother had thrown them in my father's compost pile.
After the compost had been used, eventually black walnut trees
started sprouting up everywhere. Yesterday, he
pulled one out of the ground to show me. The nut
itself was still there, split open, roots dangling from it.
As he stood there, I couldn't help noticing
just how incredibly thin he has become. He told me
his friend had died some months ago from a stroke.
I had put the trees on the floor of my car, each potted
in its own paper cup. He gave me other plants too,
along with a huge bunch of beautiful tall wildflowers
in a plastic bucket of water. My father considers them
nothing but weeds. Whatever he
gives me I stick in the ground or in vases, and
if it lives, it lives. As for the black walnut trees,
in all likelihood I won't be around long enough
to see them mature into anything meaningful.
In the not too distant future, old age will force me
to go into hiding.

OUT IN THE LATE OCTOBER GARDEN

Out in the late October garden, my father says he has been careful
not to disturb the raised beds when spreading new fertilizer.
He doesn't want to destroy the tunnels of the worms, his precious,
dear sweet worms which he depends on for aerating the soil.
He reminds me to take some wood, the locust, when I'm leaving,
since he has more than he can use and it's aged and ready to go.
He says there is also quite a bit of Chinese cabbage, and this,
along with the wood, I'm more than happy to accept. It seems
I'm always unaware of what exactly is growing in the garden.
I wouldn't blink if I were handed a basket of mangoes,
papaya and passion fruit. While I am out in the garage,
washing my hands before my father comes in, my mother slips
a hundred dollar bill into my shirt pocket for my birthday.
Since early childhood, I have had a fear of growing old, so
she knows not to make a big fuss over my being a year older.
When she returns to the kitchen, I tell the cat about the woman
I slept with last night on the other side of the river. But
it ignores me, licking its paw and letting its eyelids fall.
I had such unsettling dreams in this strange woman's bed.
I barely slept, and at dawn I could feel her sharp tailbone
pressing into my thigh as I was waiting for her to wake.
When my father enters the garage, immediately he pulls me
closer to the door, as though providing us with more privacy,
and in a deep awestruck whisper he lets me know that
he had spotted two walking sticks out on the woodpile,
mating.

MT. T HAIKU

Around the new bulb
the poet screwed in-
haiku flutter

In the warm bathroom
ladybugs fleeing from winter
die in the shower

Like the soft feathers
lining a wren's nest-
her intimate voice

Still in bed-
I stare at the ceiling
trying to make a squashed bug move

To screaming children
the dragonfly's wings
are two feet long

Mosquito
on a watermelon-
it wastes such precious time

Crows
On the side of the road
as though waiting for a ride

A goldfish stares at me-
lost in thought
I pull at chest hairs

The poor fly's coffin-
nothing more than a tissue
balled up in the trash.

FROM ROCK TO ROCK

It is only the third week in February and already the pussy willows
  at the side of the house are starting to grow soft and fat and silver.
  But it is cold in the house, as it has been cold for most of the winter.
Only when someone is visiting is it warm, since that is the only time
  I'll turn the heat up and build a fire. It doesn't happen often, though,
  that someone will visit. The winter was swallowed whole by solitude.
At times it is a joyous state to live in, at others I am reduced
  to grief and loneliness and I conclude that I live an empty life.
  When joyous I go whistling and watering from plant to plant.
When grief-stricken I care little whether the plants live or die.
  At the kitchen table, I drink cup after cup of tea, scribbling
  in small green notebooks. Much time passes between women.
This afternoon solitude took a grim turn, so I started walking
  across the field, mindlessly, but very soon it proved too muddy
  to continue and I had to abandon the goal of reaching
the edge of the woods. It was not quite plain what I had in mind, once
  I had reached there. Perhaps I could have made some minor repairs
  on the stonewall. Or perhaps a walk up the stream
would have been perfect, stepping carefully from rock to rock, staying
  as much in the center as possible.
  This has always proved to be
a very healthy exercise.

ONLY FOR THE OLD AND THE FRAGILE

I don't know why I want to live to be an old man, but I find that I do.
 It seems odd to me, when I really think about it. There is not much
 I want to accomplish. No major goals have made themselves
known to me. I cannot see myself solving any of the serious problems
 facing this race of humans that I've somehow become part of.
 That sounds condescending, and I am sorry. I want to love
another woman, create more poems and, like some other poets I know,
 I want to drink many more glasses of wine. At the end of it all,
 dying a gracious death might prove to be a worthwhile act.
And just once I would like to be able to charm the birds
 out of the trees. I have heard it said that certain people can do this,
 and these people are spoken of with very noticeable envy.
I would be grateful if the birds were to come down
 and land on my shoulders. If I were an old man, I would be thin
 and weightless and these birds would pick me up and carry me away.
They would also be kind enough to pick up my wife also.
 We would float in the air like people in a painting by Chagall.
 For this, I would want to live to be an old man. I have no desire
to accumulate wealth, and fame is completely out of the question.
 That the birds should hold me aloft, that would be all I would ask for.
 Birds do this only for the old and the fragile.

VERTICAL BRANCHES

While she is upstairs taking a morning bath, I walk to the diner,
  and knowing just how long it takes her to bathe, I won't need
to hurry back. I take a newspaper and coffee and sit at
one of the many empty booths. I find the sports section to be
  the best appetizer when it comes to making my way through
  a newspaper. This diner is a morning gathering place
for carpenters, electricians and plumbers. They find comfort in
  rubbing their lives up close to one another. But since it is Sunday
  there are only two men sitting at the counter. They are immersed
in eating egg sandwiches the gods would kill for. I resist ordering one
  for myself, since having breakfast together on Sunday is
  a supreme ritual my girlfriend will not do without. I can tell you,
a meal far more ambitious than egg sandwiches will be prepared.
  Autumn has come to a rapid conclusion. Intense rain and winds
  have swept the trees clean of the most stubborn of leaves.
In the window, next to the booth which I share with ghosts and a fly,
  towering branches of poplar trees block any view of the mountains.
  You'd think branches pointing so steeply upwards would be unsuitable
for perching, but as I sip my coffee I notice many birds in these trees.
  The older of the two men (I could spend the rest of my days
  simply eavesdropping), who is very heavy and who has nonetheless
somehow managed to live to a ripe old age, is reading the obituaries.
  In a loud voice he claims that people are dying to get their names
  in the newspaper. The other man totally ignores this remark,
most likely because this same old man makes this same remark
  every Sunday morning. Then, after a brief pause, the old man
  squeezes more ketchup onto his egg sandwich.
The other man suddenly grunts in agreement,
  as he turns his eyes upwards to look out at the birds
  that mysteriously continue to choose vertical branches
  to perch on.

SCREW DARLING

we'd better
screw darling

we'd better
butter the sheets

crank up
the golden fan

give ourselves
our unholy all

before ant hills
get way too tall.

DUST AND ASHES

As can only be expected, I am losing the eternal battle
  against dust and ashes. Dust seems able to accumulate
  wherever it has a mind to. Just when I think I have managed
to get it under control, it shows me just how very wrong I am
  by parading out new armies that far exceed in volume
  anything I thought I might be able to reasonably deal with.
I should be used to it by now; it has always been this way.
  And the ashes, existing in perfect communion with dust, they
  possess an amazing talent for migrating to other rooms to take up
permanent residence. It seems I'm always cleaning out the fireplace,
  carrying buckets of ashes out to the edge of the woods.
  Then (god forbid I should overlook them) there are the
very exquisite ashes from the incense that is always burning.
  These are especially challenging to dispose of. It's like attempting to
  gather up the extra-fine remains of shadows that have been cremated.
But, for some reason, I never bother cleaning the room I write in,
  where I sit at the window facing the mountains to the west.
  Dust and ashes seem appropriate in here. The ashtray, for example,
is usually overflowing with huge turd-shaped ashes that have fallen
  from cigars. It's a dirty habit, I know. It's only that the cigar does
  such an excellent job of absorbing the tension in my jaws.
It's a tension that sets in when I realize, once again, that
  I have nothing very meaningful to write, that little
  beyond dust and ashes is worth any serious mention.

DEATH POEMS

Every day comes down to the moment
When a poet should write a death poem

And every day this death poem should be
Destroyed, rolled up
Into a ball and set on fire,
Maybe in a large clay bowl

And at least once a week this bowl
Should be emptied, the ashes thrown out
The back door into the wind and rain and
Snow, into the sunlight which is sometimes
As gray
As ashes
And just as soft.

VISITING MY GRANDMOTHER

Every spring we would drive to Pennsylvania to visit
my mother's mother. Before the interstate highway came
into existence it would take a good twelve hours to make this trip.
As a kid, I felt as though we were driving around the world.
One evening, arriving at my grandmother's house, I felt sick as a dog.
To help remedy this condition, my father pulled a bottle
of blackberry brandy out of the glove compartment and instructed me
to take a couple of big swallows. Needless to say, very quickly
and very gloriously I got drunk as a skunk, which was exactly
the goal my father had had in mind. I was carried away and deposited
in my grandmother's bed, of all places. I tried to tell my father
that this arrangement would only make matters worse, but
it was like talking to a shovel. The idea of sleeping in my
grandmother's bed made me squeamish and almost nauseous.
Never was there a woman who looked more like an old world peasant
than my grandmother did. The fear haunted me that someday
my mother would resemble her. I had suspicions that
when my grandmother was over seventy she had given birth
to my mother in a hen house. True, she had the kindest,
the most loving eyes you could ever imagine encountering on this cold,
barbaric planet, but that didn't soften the shock of where
my sick belly and I had ended up. But, if the truth
must be told, once I was tucked into the sheets, that
smelled from walnuts and lilacs and flour, I was just fine.
The pillow had enough feathers stuffed in it to keep a dozen chickens
warm during a sudden surprise snowfall in April. Even so,
the next night I was very happy to find myself in
one of the beds that was usually kept fresh for visitors.
That was the night my little sister was crying her eyes out,
my mother and father having gone off to a barn dance with a flock
of relatives crammed into one car. Everyone had gone except
my grandmother and my Uncle George. He was a tall, gaunt,
speechless individual who always looked as though he were
listening to someone whisper naughty things in his ear. Like
my grandmother, though, he was a kind and gentle person,
and when he heard my sister crying he took his violin out
of a closet and he started playing a melody that was so tender
that she almost immediately fell off to sleep. In the middle
of that same night, my father helping my sister out of bed
awakened me. Somehow she had successfully conveyed to him
that she had to use the outhouse. He was wearing
my uncle's miner's hat that cast a very strong beam.
Through the bedroom window, I could see him escorting her
through the enormous darkness of the Pennsylvania night.
Solemnly, they walked hand-in-hand, as though leaving
on a pilgrimage from which they might never return.

BETWEEN BEDS

I shouldn't be walking
across this frozen lake.
The ice is so pitifully thin
I might fall right through.
Also, I'm afraid that the
delicate cracking sounds
are going to wake the birds
which like to sleep late
on such cold mornings. Certainly,
they do not care that I am
taking this shortcut home.
They do not care that I am
drunk at dawn, that I am traveling
between beds, that the bed
at my destination
is the empty one.

FAREWELL

A light frosting of snow this morning.
  I threw apples out for the deer, not
  from the kindness of my heart but
because I didn't care to eat them myself.
  Actually, I haven't seen a deer out back
  since late autumn, some three weeks ago.
A gnawing sense of grief has taken hold of my gut.
  I don't want to leave for work. I feel like
  a child being sent off to school, and this child
wants nothing more than to remain at home,
  to play with his tin castle and colorful knights.
  To this day, I can remember the last time
I did play with them, when I had the sad
  realization that I was getting too old.
  I can still feel it. This I can never see
happening with poetry, since the writing
  of a poem has always been, for me, the
  simple rehearsal of writing that last note
  of farewell,
  on my deathbed.

DEVOURING BIRDS

My father never expressed good memories of childhood,
and because of this he thought it only reasonable that
his own children shouldn't have any either. Adding to this,
my mother had the annoying habit of reminding us that
my father never wanted to have children in the first place.
Sometimes I would wonder how on earth she could make
such a crazy statement, but then my father would do something
that would prove her remark sane. When around age seven,
I had a dream of my father taking an axe and chopping
our dog's head off. I woke from this dream in horror and
I went looking for the poor dog's dead body, only to find it
dozing beneath the Christmas tree. It looked at me as if to say,
"Relax, things are not as bad as you seem to think."
Not long after that, the dog died of old age. My mother
had taken it to the vet, and later that evening he gave us
a call to give us the news. We never collected the ashes.
Back in those days, we had numerous pets and if we had
kept the ashes of every one that had died there would've
been cans of ashes everywhere. A dead fish, we would flush
down the toilet. I remember, this one time, my little sister and
I solemnly standing over a small, bright red fish floating in the toilet,
paying credence to the woeful fact that it had had only one life; and
that this life had been spent in a tank in a kitchen, watching a family
of five thriving humans devouring birds and cows and pigs.
None of our cats had had more than one life. Every August,
it seemed, we would find one or two of them dead, still wearing their
pathetic little boots. Then there was the time my father brought home
a baby alligator, a souvenir from my fat Aunt Helen's Florida vacation.
No one had to tell us that while she was there she had soaked up more
sunlight than a grove of magnificent oranges. Coming face to face with
this alligator, my mother panicked, screamed her head off
and went running through the house as though it was on fire.
We put the alligator in the bathtub where, overnight, doubt had grown
in its chest. The next morning, in the driveway,
my father drenched it in gasoline and then threw a burning
match on it, heaving the match as though it was a tiny harpoon.
When a green smoke cleared, he swept the ashes out onto a road
that led to eternity and, hopefully, to a tenderness as yet unheard of.

IN THE FACE OF THINGS

In the cold of an April afternoon
I tie a rope between two trees

and hang my clothes out to dry.
I sit in the rusty green lawn chair

and sip red wine, watching my
shirt flapping like an old flag.

I see a bird land on the rope and it
starts frantically pecking at this shirt.

So I pick up a stick, one which had fallen
from my arms when bringing in wood,

and I throw it at the bird. It flies away,
no doubt to add some blue threads to its nest.

I sip my wine and wish it a long and happy life,
even though it has left me with that much less

of a shirt to protect myself from the cold wind
that comes off the river; a cold wind demanding

that somehow I be that much more gracious and
that much more understanding in the face of things.

THE MARCH SUN

In this cold valley, in this house that is impossible to keep warm,
  the greatest pleasure these winter days and nights, comes from
  simply standing in the shower and allowing hot water to rain
down upon me.   And I find it's best to allow the bathroom to get
  so steamy that it's almost impossible to locate the doorknob,
  then I have enough courage to eventually leave the bathroom.
Yesterday I found myself taking two showers. I took one
  in the morning and then one when I came back from
  my afternoon walk by the lake, where I see the same man fishing
in the same hole almost every day. Once I waved to him and
  I ended up walking out onto the frozen lake to talk to him, where
  he stood with his dog. The dog was white and it sat there
as though frozen to the ice. I asked him what the dog's name was,
  and he told me it was Mr. Pierre. I wondered where
  Mrs. Pierre was and what she might be stuck to, but
I refrained from asking. This simple brief conversation made me
  feel as though I owed myself at least half a dozen especially long
  hot steamy showers. When my lover came back from Morocco,
I couldn't believe my eyes when they fell on her tanned flesh.
  Agape, I wondered what sun was capable of bringing about
  such a total and miraculous transformation.
Here, the sun crosses the sky, most days, undetected,
  shrouded by gray clouds as firmly locked in place as Mr. Pierre.
  When it is detected it is largely ignored.
 It is a god without a people.

THE CLAY PIG AND REMEMBERED PRAYERS

I put the clay pig that my lover brought back for me from Morocco,
on the mantelpiece with the other pigs which have come to me
over the years. This clay pig is especially striking, so exquisitely
crude and bold is it. Perhaps it is because I was born in the year
of the pig that so many pigs have managed to somehow gather
on my mantelpiece. I don't know. From what I hear, the pig is
supposed to bring good luck. That being the case, it is fortunate
that I have so many. Soon I will be on the wrong side of fifty,
without a penny in the bank, only a few thin sticks of furniture
to my name and a body that aches if a breeze moves a hair on it.
It is glaringly obvious that I'm going to need all the good luck
that these pigs can possibly supply. I did notice, though, that
after my lover gave me the pig she became very ill, unable
to get out of bed for days. Her voice was so weary she could
barely speak a word. I brought soup to her house, which is
located on the other side of the wide river that separates us.
I even went so far as to suggest that maybe I should bring
the pig back to her, that maybe her giving it to me was just
too severe a blow to her own fortunes. After all, she too
was born in the year of the pig, just as I was. She refused
my offer, looking at me as though she were dealing with
a person gone a bit haywire. I'm happy to report, though,
that bringing her the soup very much pleased her.
It was a navy bean and tomato concoction, which took
precious little time to prepare. Other than the stale parsley,
I had considered flavoring it with a ham hock, thinking
this would give it a more substantial, heart-warming flavor.
But on further, careful consideration I abandoned this idea,
suspecting she might be repulsed by the taste of animal.
Instead, when finished making the soup, I simply dunked
the clay pig in it a couple of times and I mumbled
parts of what I could remember of some boyhood prayers.

THE WILD MOUSE AND THE EXPLODING CIGAR

For a week, in the summertime, we would stay at the Jersey shore.
    First thing, after checking in at a motel and unloading the car,
  we'd play miniature golf on the little green course located on top
of a building that housed the usual shops found along the boardwalk.
  It was beautiful up there, a bit sleazy but sublime because of
  a breathtaking view of the ocean. Happiness was ours on that day,
relishing the fact that a whole week of vacation was rolled out before us,
    and there was always the hope that it might never come to an end.
  At least once, during this magical stay, my little sister and I would
find the courage to ride the Wild Mouse. This frightening thing thrived
    at the end of a narrow pier of lights and frenzy. We feared
  that this insane contraption was long overdue to collapse and plunge
into the ocean, taking its victims to the bottom of a murky watery hell.
  Whenever I think back on those summers
  I wonder if the Wild Mouse is still there, still torturing children
screaming for dear life. The reason we persisted, through the years,
    in confronting this tormenting force, was because we believed that
  we actually greatly benefited from the experience. When our
yearly ride was over we felt free and brave and toughened up,
    as though it would now be a snap to face the terrors of another year
  of childhood. I never felt any doubt that other children had the
same reaction to surviving this ride. As for my parents, other than
    strolling the boardwalk and staring out at the end of the world, eyes
  afloat in peace and resignation, they did not do much. My
little sister and I were always at wit's end, wondering how we might
    liven up our subdued party of four. Our very favorite prank, the one
  most often resorted to, was to booby trap one of my father's cigars.
We purchased the tiny explosives at one of the local magic shops.
  The actual preparation of the cigar required much patience, since
  the explosives had to be well hidden inside it, and neither
the cigar nor the paper it was wrapped in could appear
  to have been tampered with. So, he'd be out there, strolling
  the boardwalk with his family, proud of the fact that in this
very difficult and challenging world he had been successful enough
  to be able to afford to show us all good time. We'd watch him
  take a cigar out of his top pocket, meticulously unwrap it,
put it in his eagerly waiting mouth, pause in his stroll, block
  the ocean breeze by striking a match in cupped hands
  and then after a couple of deeply satisfying puffs: kaboom!
Immediately my little sister and I would be swept away
  by hysterical gales of laughter. My father, he would
  waste no time in throwing one of his classic tantrums,
something that happened all too often, even over matters far less
    alarming than an exploding cigar. Now, the secret
  of blunting such an eruption depended on my not showing any fear.
This, as you can well imagine, was not so easy to do.

Showing fear could cause a storm of raw physical abuse to rain down
upon me (something my sisters were never subjected to).
It was best to just stand there, as though with
   some small measure of tranquility I was looking at
 a tornado in the distance, and I was confident in the belief
that it was moving in the direction of a town
   other than the one I was living in. As soon as possible
   the laughing would come to an end. Laughing
was a risky thing to indulge in too freely. The only place
   laughter was accepted was in front of the television set.
 Violence could take place anywhere at anytime,
but laughter should be directed only at comedians,
   such as when Bob Hope was entertaining the troops.
   Bob Hope was getting paid to be laughed at, whereas
my father was not (so he had the habit of reminding us,
   from time to time).

A BLACK DOG PLAYING IN THE SNOW

My mother hands me a vodka and lemonade and I am shocked
at how strong it is. There exists barely a trace of lemonade in it.
We drink two each, then sit down to have dinner with my father.
I always thought my mother would outlive my father, until about
two years ago, when he started showing signs of Alzheimer's.
There was that one gray autumn afternoon in particular, which
I recall so clearly. It was a cold autumn afternoon and there
were a lot of crows in the yard taking the old bread my mother
had thrown out, and on that cold day, my father kept endlessly
repeating the same insignificant dry piece of information having
to do with his black check book. It was on that day that we knew
with rancid horrid certainty that he was a victim of this disease. Now,
a brutal irony has become very apparent:
my father very well might outlive my mother.
The man eats like a horse, sleeps like a baby, and a
strange calmness has come over him, a warm-hearted
calmness of spirit which is something he simply did not
have before; whereas my mother has lost twenty pounds,
cannot sleep at night and in general is a total nervous wreck.
She has become a frayed and withered shadow of her old self.
When his brain was healthy, he'd constantly be looking out at
the garden while we were having a meal, as though he wanted
to escape from the emotional responsibilities of a family by fleeing to
his hot house. Now he never looks out there, and if he does he'll,
more often than not, experience hallucinations that almost lift him out
of his skin. Whenever this happens he'll quickly turn to his family
as though seeking refuge. Today, when he looked out at the garden
he saw a black dog playing in the snow, and there was neither a dog
nor snow out there. I realized that a man in his condition, arriving
at a Nazi concentration camp, would face immediate extermination.

FIRES

Word has come to the house that a pyromaniac is on the loose.
   Yesterday alone three fires were reported in the area, although
   none was close to the house. With the way the wind

has been behaving of late, a fire many thousands of acres away
   could easily reach us. True, we do not own this house, but
   it is home and it is filled with our belongings. The last fire

which came close, within a hundred yards, left the landscape
   reduced to a great ashen garden. We've considered leaving,
   to allow the landlord to rent to less fearful people.

But, in all likelihood, that would mean returning to the city
   and we refuse to entertain that thought. The violence
   of where we would have to resort to living would be more,

at this time in life, than we could tolerate. At least here
   we have a chance of fleeing with advanced warning, whereas
   in the city violence strikes without warning. Also, here we can be

saved by rain, if it ever decides to return. Thunderstorms happen,
   but not often enough to bring meaningful relief from the dryness.
   We were told before coming here that it might be like this.

We did not pay much attention to this warning,
   having had no experience with fires so breathtaking and wild.
   Often I'll be at one of the windows peering out into the woods,

looking for signs of smoke. My wife tells me that I am becoming
   obsessive. We've decided on which belongings
   we would save in a last minute dash to the car.

The list is kept on the refrigerator door, held there by a magnet,
   right next to a photo taken, last winter,
   of the back field covered with peaceful snow.

CATALOGUE OF THE DOGS

The warm smiling dogs of twinkling compassion
  have since the day of birth only one coat each,
  and this they find unfortunate since they have
  no coats to share with the shivering multitudes.
The foul smelling somber dogs of rainy days
  find refuge in the empty chamber of a shrine where,
  mistaken for some of the many sacrificial animals,
  they meet their deaths in an extravagant show of ritual.
The famished yet patient dogs of frozen pizza
  stare into a decaying oven in a small town in Iowa,
  as the evening sun glows red behind a lowly hill
  covered with leafless black trees.
The dogs of unbaptized children
  worry night and day that the angel of death
  might exhibit an appetite for easy prey.
The dogs of August
  stroll in the garden, as their heavy tongues droop
  and drool on the precious blessings of summer.
The dogs of pride
  grow blind.
The casual shiny dogs of Christmas
  cannot make toys and cannot fly, content rather
  to stay at home to beg fresh baked cookies from the Mrs.
The frozen dogs of midnight silence
  sniff at their own breath
  when it rises before them.
The miserable dogs of poetry
  are tied to the back porch every night,
  where they resort to eating rodents
  and where they die very young.
The dogs of the Acropolis lie under the sacred olive tree,
  as unfazed by tourists as bones are unfazed by death.
The dogs of countless sheep
  doze off on the job.
The dogs of envy
  choke to death when swallowing
  the smiles of their enemies.
The faithful joyous dogs of St. Francis
  somehow manage to exist on the crumbs of bread
  thrown to birds.
The dogs that sneak into the church,
  to steal holy water on a sultry July afternoon,
  are the same dogs that sit in the priest's black car
  every Monday night, waiting for him to finish bowling.
The dogs that ate bullfrogs for dinner
  are made miserable by having to listen
  to the bullfrogs' ghosts croaking all night long.
The dogs that went frolicking far into the evil dark woods
  are the dead dogs that had their tongues
  strangled and stuffed down their throats.

The dogs back from participating in the firefly hunt
  are stretched out, blissfully snoozing on
  the back porch from which you can hear
  a ball game on the small radio, broadcast
  from a faraway place called Cleveland.
The dogs of anger
  want to chew on
  greedy tyrants.
The hacking cursed dogs of limbo
  pace back and forth, obliterating their own tracks,
  nails growing longer and longer, sinking deeper
  and deeper into warm soft ashes.
The baggy dogs of Babe Ruth
  are lucky if a single morsel of hot dog bun
  is thrown their way, and have long since
  abandoned the hope of ever tasting
  any of the meat.
The panting dogs of astonishing Marilyn Monroe
  fetch her slippers, lick her feet and then fall
  asleep in her closet among fallen dresses.
The dogs of fame
  fetch roses.
The dogs of romance
  fetch Joe.
The dogs of suicide
  fetch pills.
The dogs of lust
  prefer their bowls of flesh
  to be forbidden.
The flesh-eating dogs of war-mongers
  get their daily fill, simply by stepping
  onto the battlefield.
The white fluffy dogs of the Alaskan wilderness
  dream of meandering across a summer sky,
  lapping up all the blue they can reach
  before outspoken black thunderstorms
  threaten to devour everything in sight.
The dogs of troubled sleep and insomnia
  walk out into the chill of dawn, unable to pick up
  the blissful scent of dew.
The dogs of Julia Child
  lick creamed black mushroom sauce
  off their noses.
The dogs of famine
  eventually eat one another,
  to no one's surprise.
The dogs of gluttony
  dwell obsessively over roasted wild boars
  so far into the night that they forget
  the weight of their own sin.

The bored-silly dogs of Pierre Bonnard
  piss on the rugs of late interiors.
The Bombay Sapphire dogs of dry gin
  cast shadows magnificent and icy
  on evening's weightier decisions.
The thousand dogs of desert alienation and lunacy
  cringe at the edge of an empty swimming pool
  like faithful servants staring into an open grave.
The confident big blonde dogs of heaven
  lie at the feet of the Almighty and
  sneeze when the Almighty sneezes
  and yawn when the Almighty yawns
  and fart blood when the Almighty farts blood.
The haggard green dogs of Christopher Columbus
  sit at ship's bow, noses pressed to the salty wind, sick of the odor
  of sweat and suspicions and grumblings both ignorant and holy,
  famished of belly and brain for fresh kill
  and the fires that make men loving again.
The dogs of avarice
  have no fixed limit to where
  they stick their noses.
The dogs of a Nantucket hotel
  whimper the loss of the proprietor,
  murdered when arguing with an angry harpooner
  who claimed he had found a live eel in his clam chowder.
O the world!
O the world!
The dogs of Mars
  exhibit glowing orange eyes
  that are so hypnotic
  the night never wants to end.
The dogs of Frankenstein
  have fur standing on end.
The dogs of the last supper
  are thrown scraps of bread
  mercifully soaked in wine.
The dogs of hell
  extol the holiday pleasures of snow.
The dogs of paradise
  extol the holiday pleasures of
  bells and kisses and perfumes
  sweetly afflicting the human heart.
The dogs of sloth
  hate hunting.
The dogs of Miguel
  talk all through the night, but
  only one of the dogs has time enough to tell
  its life story.

LEAVE YOUR SORROW

Leave your sorrow
at the bird sanctuary.

Leave your sorrow
there for the birds

to make nests and
to make songs from it.

The birds will turn
your sorrow into new life.

They will turn your sorrow
into songs of such purity

that you will not recognize
your sorrow when

you again return
to the bird sanctuary.

LOST IN SPACE

My older sister sang in the choir. We would attend Christmas Eve mass and she'd be up there with the other girls surrounding the organ, and she would be singing her precious little golden heart out and it would be a very special night. I wanted to be an altar boy, but the Latin proved too intimidating, meager as it was. Somehow I ended up working in the basement of the church along with my good friend Charlie. I cannot recall exactly what our responsibilities were, but I know we never put any true measure of seriousness into them. Periodically we would break into the supply of Holy Communion wafers and snack on them as though they were potato chips. The wafers, not yet consecrated, we figured we were committing no great sin. When they were consecrated, the priest would place one on my boyhood tongue on a Sunday morning. Without fail, once back kneeling in the pew, the wafer would get stuck to the roof of my mouth. So, there I was, crowded into a pew,
my fish eyes staring blindly at the ceiling, and on the roof of my mouth was stuck the body and blood of Christ being abused by my frantic, sinful tongue. Oftentimes this would throw me into such a state of panic that I'd faint and have to be carried out of the church by other boys. I would be deposited on the steps like a drunk who had been thrown out of a tavern. In those days the emergency squad was never called. A nun would hand me a glass of cold water, and when it was decided that I had regained my equilibrium I was then allowed to walk home. Honestly, at that point I felt as though I had just successfully risen from the dead. On those walks home, the birds sounded brighter and more cheerful and they, I'm sure, looked upon me as being a newly liberated soul, as though I had become one of them. Anyway, Charlie used to have this theory about the nature of time in connection with God. His simple claim was that time was God and God was time. He never said anything about space or matter. To Charlie, time was eternal and every moment was eternal time, and that being the case he wanted to get laid. His mission was to get laid so that the moment of getting laid would last for all eternity. It was all such pure, such beautiful, such enthusiastic nonsense that I said nothing to refute even a fraction of his theory. Besides, I liked his enthusiasm. It was infectious, filled with mirth and, hell, he wouldn't tolerate questions anyway. He would point to his watch and say that it's time to get laid. One day, the nun who worked down in the basement with us, caught us snacking on the Holy Communion wafers and talking about getting laid for all eternity. Well, yeah, she smacked us around, a good sound smacking it was, smacked us right silly. Walking home that cheerless afternoon in frosty autumn, I told Charlie that

from now on when we were working in the basement of the church he should keep his mouth shut about getting laid.

In an attempt to make sense to him, I told him that because of his freaking stupid big mouth we'd now be getting smacked around by a nun for all eternity. Of course, my words had zero effect on his behavior. He simply revised his theory about time and God, claiming that God only remembered the good moments and that only these good moments lasted for all eternity. Eventually the bad moments were forgotten and they turned into dust and got lost in space.

SNOWY MORNINGS

My father never showed much affection for my mother, primarily
  because my mother discouraged him from doing so, at least when
we kids were around. It was on snowy mornings, when my mother
was not present, that I heard my father speak words of passion.
  These words, along with much caressing, he directed at his car.
On those mornings he'd be pressed up against the wheel, cajoling his
1955 red Ford wagon up that steep slippery road nearby our house,
  which had to be taken so we could get to school and he to his job. Only
  the very worst of storms would warrant us staying home from school,
and even those wouldn't keep my father home. We would creep up that
  snowy hill in his honey of a car, that car that was like the other woman
  in his life. He'd be saying stuff like, "Come on, baby, you can do it, you
can do it, baby, come on sweetheart, o that's my pretty sweetheart."
  He'd be rubbing and caressing the steering wheel, leaning up close to it
  as though any second he was going to plant a big tender kiss right on
the dashboard. Eventually, from all his cajoling and caressing, and with
  the help of whatever angels were out working the early morning hours,
  we would reach the top of the hill. Once there he would gasp and swoon
with relief and pleasure and we kids would just sit there wide-eyed with
  astonishment and wonder, not fully understanding anything.
For myself, I knew that someday I wanted to experience whatever
it was my father had just experienced. I wanted to know that
  same sense of ecstatic relief. I wanted this to happen to me
  untold thousands of times. From simply watching the pleasure
he had derived from our brief journey, desire had taken hold of me.
  But until old enough to actually experience the ecstasy of driving
  through snow, I knew I would have to be content with whatever
my budding imagination could supply me in a closed garage.
  One evening, when I thought I would not be noticed, I slipped out
  to the garage and got into the car. I positioned myself behind
the wheel and I caressed it with what I thought was a passion
  equal in power and duration to what my father had exhibited.
  But, no matter how much I concentrated, nothing happened.
I knew only the loneliness of sitting in a car that was going nowhere
  on an evening when no one seemed to miss me. In defeat,
  I closed my eyes and sleep came over me. In a dream
I saw a lion turn into a tall lily that turned into the wind.
When I woke, the garage was dark as a miner's lung and cold as ice,
and I could hear a high piercing sound.
I knew that at the back door of the house
my father was whistling for me to come in.

ZORRO

At one point in my childhood, I had to watch every episode of Zorro.
There was something in the character that I strongly identified with.
Perhaps it was the fact that this man, defender of the people against
villains and unjust officials, was living a lie whether wearing his mask
or not. The Lone Ranger did not live a lie. He was always
the Lone Ranger, always in mask. He wore it
sitting around the campfire, eating pork and beans,
bathing in the river, when mopping the sweat off Silver.
The first thing Tonto saw upon waking, when he rolled over
in the morning, was the mask. Tonto did not know this man as
anyone other than the Lone Ranger. But Zorro led two lives,
one making a lie of the other. My parents, who were fully aware
of my addiction to Zorro on TV, did not consider this harmful.
In fact, on one of my birthdays my father got it into his head to
give me a Zorro costume. I was thrilled beyond belief. Every night
after dinner I would put on my black cape, my black hat, grab hold
of my black whip and I'd disappear out the back door into the
adventuresome dark, into whatever woods were still remaining in
the neighborhood. My immediate destination was usually the tree
right outside Mrs. Hoffmann's bathroom window. I felt free
from my other self, the self that had to endure the boredom of school,
the claustrophobia of church, the tyranny of my father. It did
bother me that my parents knew that I was Zorro. I felt that
if I could have deceived them, I would have been the happiest
of all masked children. As time went on, though, the suspicion grew
in me that my father had made a gift of this costume simply because
he wanted me to disappear. It became all too obvious
that that was the reason why, every night, he held the door wide open
as I dashed out into the big dark to once again do battle with the evils
and the injustices of the world. At least that had been the impression
I wanted to give.

SAY A PRAYER FOR MY DOG

At 89 my father is hospitalized with an infection of the bladder
and, while there, other complications develop. My mother and I travel
through bitter cold wintry weather to visit him. We take the elevator up
to the 4th floor, not knowing what to expect. I try to prepare my mother
for the worst. Today we find him skinny and twisted and mangled and,
except for catheter and a blue plastic diaper, totally naked.
I'm amazed at how prehistoric his feet look, as though they are turning
into claws. He babbles and points a curled finger at
the waxen light in the window, a light that seems bored and impersonal.
My mother and I are too numb to speak. The fear comes over me that,
soon enough, I will be in my father's place. I start dwelling
on my own death. I notice the other bed in the room is empty, waiting.
But I'm saved from my thoughts when the nurse comes in and says
that my father needs something to drink, if only to lessen his dryness.
She pushes a button and the bed starts making a tortured,
hideously whining sound as the upper part of his body rises. She
hands me a milk carton that looks as though it's for a school child.
It has a straw sticking out of it. I place the straw in his mouth
and nothing happens. The nurse speaks to him in a kind voice and
a tender voice and finally he takes a couple of sips. Then he
turns his head away, mouth hanging open. His tongue is white
from dryness and milk. He started life's journey drinking milk
and now, as he nears the end, he is back to drinking milk. Often
he laments that he wants nothing but for this journey to be over.
He is weary, and beyond the fact that he dearly loves my mother
he cannot see any reason for living anymore.
His very robust, healthy disgust for life is nothing new.
When we were kids, my younger sister and I would laugh
in a restaurant when he would order Coconut Custard Pie.
We thought he was ordering Coconut Disgusted Pie. He stares
at the waxen light in the window, that light that seems numb
and bored yet wants to say something about milk and death.
When we are leaving, attempting to convey our good-byes,
he reaches out and grabs my wrist. He pulls me close to him,
and in my ear he mumbles, "Say a prayer for my dog."

BEFORE ALZHEIMER'S

As I'm setting the table I hear my father reminding himself
to call the principal's office to report that, because of a toothache,
he will not be able to attend school in the morning. In the kitchen,
dimly lit as though by tiny white flames that are nearing exhaustion,
we talk about his 90th birthday party, which we are planning for June
and which he seems very pleased with. Before Alzheimer's, as far back
as I can remember, my father and I had little in common; but
now he has become gentle and considerate, even philosophical,
and his approaching death has brought us closer to one another.
I find myself aspiring to be like him. Perhaps because I am a poet
I talk about death more than most people are willing to indulge in,
and such talk has always brought about disgruntlement in my father.
Now we have this topic in common, and we do not forget to
make good use of it every chance we get. Before Alzheimer's
he'd have never entertained, for a second, the thought of there
being a party in his honor. Whenever he does suspect something
is wrong with himself, and this does happen, he'll gaze and babble
in wonderment and in dread. Then there are times when he displays
remnants of his old self. Just this morning he devoured much of what
was in the bag of pastries I had picked up at the bakery,
ignoring the tooth he had claimed had started aching him
during the night. I couldn't help remembering those Sundays,
when I was a kid, when without fail he'd bring home, after church,
a big joyous bag of cream doughnuts and jelly doughnuts.
On one such Sunday, late in the evening when he was hypnotized
by television, I took one of the doughnuts and I poured half a bottle
of my mother's perfume into it. Then I stationed myself at the table,
as though doing homework, and I waited. Eventually, when
a commercial broke the spell he was under, he came into the kitchen
and chose that doughnut; and I watched, after tip-toeing after him, as
with remarkable satisfaction he sat back down in front of the television
and he ate the doughnut as though it was the last doughnut in the world.

BIRD ALONE

I sit in the world and I am writing a poem, after many decades
of reading countless other poems. At this point it seems like
an absurd thing to do, that maybe it would make more sense to
simply sit here and watch the people walking by the movie theater
that has been turned into a taxi stand. Red and green neon lights
in the window of the Chinese restaurant have just come on.
Birds are singing their evening songs, something poets are prone to
notice and mention. But the birds are so many and their songs
all sound the same to me, just as I sound like most other poets.
This is a realization that causes a deep ache in my soul, but I cannot
let this keep me from writing countless new poems.
Without the writing of poems life would lose purpose.
The other day my lover complained to me that I had not
written a love poem for her in ages. Here was someone
in need of a poem from me, a very rare occurrence. This
made me very happy. Usually I feel like a bird alone in a tree,
my songs dead leaves falling quietly to earth. I am a bird alone,
a cold wind separating my feathers, and I am singing when perhaps
I should be observing silence and my head should be stuffed down into
my soft warm shoulders. Yes, I am a bird with shoulders, and I am tired
of looking at my beak. It never changes its expression, no matter
how much I sing my little heart out.

YEAR AFTER YEAR

Friends visit and tell me the house is too large for one person,
  that the walls need to be painted and I should get some furniture
  so the place doesn't look so empty. And how, in god's name,
can I enjoy a fire on a cold winter night when there is nothing
  to sit on in front of the fireplace? I tell them that I sit leaning up
  against the wall and that I am perfectly comfortable. I notice
that no one is quick to accept an invitation to share a fire late at night.
  The only crowded room has the typewriter in it.
  This room overflows with wooden animals, skulls from real animals,
statues, books and music. Paintings and photos cover
  the walls, also poems from favorite poets including
  Issa, Parra and Carruth. The largest photograph is
of Forbes Field, the first night game ever played on June 4th, 1940,
  between Pittsburgh and Boston. Pittsburgh won 14 to 2.
  Strings of tiny white lights hang in the windows.
These lights outline one window, in the other window,
  the one facing the road, lights hang in the shape of a cross.
  If it were not for the massive oak in the front yard,
you'd be able to see the mailbox on the other side of the road.
  When you live alone, year after year, you dwell on every detail.
  There's an ancient lawn chair at the back door, where I like to read.
The seat is eaten away by rust, so when I sit on it
  half my ass falls through. The birds, among their loved ones,
  are not aware of this.

CHARLIE

My best friend, Charlie, lived down by the river, his house
only a couple of blocks away from where I lived. Mornings,
we'd walk to school together, then back home in the afternoon.
On the way to school, Charlie would coach me on the homework
I had ignored doing the night before, then on the way home we'd
talk jazz, spy novels, girls we thought we might be able to entice
into his gray Studebaker that was forever up on blocks in his driveway.
Life was carefree, uncomplicated, we were not yet aware of the shadow
of death hanging over us. Except for that one morning, when a couple
of local toughs came up to us and started pushing Charlie around.
He had made the dumb mistake of becoming sweet on the wrong
beautiful girl with red hair, a mistake which the two toughs intended to
make Charlie pay for. They said little before beating my dear friend
to a pulp. What could I do, but simply stand there and watch, acting
as though I had no idea who this Charlie person was. I figured that
if I had jumped into the fray, I too would have ended up on the ground
with fists pummeling my poor helpless skinny body, that always
had the smell of crushed dandelions about it, even in the depths of winter.
When it was over and the toughs had swaggered and sauntered off,
Charlie managed to stand on his quivering feet and continue our walk
home from school. He showed no disappointment or anger towards me.
He knew I could never have saved him, and he accepted this. And
being the smart fellow that he was, he was also not unaware that he
would've behaved likewise had it been I who had been on the ground
receiving such brutal treatment. This understanding did nothing
to tarnish our friendship, and perhaps it even served to strengthen
the bond between us. What also enhanced the bond between us,
strangely enough, was the total absence of any qualms about fighting one
another. In the heat of an argument, neither of us would
shy away from physical violence. Confronting one another, there was no
limit to how brave we could be. We'd become the most
capable of warriors, and without much provocation or hesitation, we'd
commence giving one another a firm thrashing. I'd beat
the living daylights out of Charlie and Charlie would do the same to me.
Such battles could go on for a frightening length of time.
We'd be staggering, wildly swinging, smashing fists
into ribs and faces, tearing at eyeballs, ripping ears off
and flattening noses. Then, hey, what else could we do
but lie down exhausted on somebody's front lawn, laughing,
talking about the leaves and the clouds and how unfortunate it was
that they had been the only witnesses of such a great battle.
And o we were so proud. We were very merry and we were very proud,
and o how brave we had been in our time of fleeting youth,
and o what glorious victories we had so fiercely accomplished.

A WOMAN SLEEPING ON THE DOCK

There is a woman sleeping on the dock, lying on her side.
  Curiosity alone makes me want to introduce myself but,
  of course, at the same time I do not want to disturb her.
I have never seen anyone sleeping on this dock before.
  A nearby picnic bench will be a good place for me to
  sit and wait for her to wake. I would like to know
who she is. Will I scare her? That is the question.
  Sure, I am a harmless old melon-headed poet, but
  she does not know this. She does not know of
the pain in my feet, that they have become clay birds
  unable to spread their wings anymore.
How long must I sit here? She does not move.
Only her hair, such fine threads of separating light,
  reacts to the breeze coming off the lake. It seems
  far too chilly for her to be comfortable, although
it is obvious that she is still a strong young woman.
  Her skin has not yet taken on that transparency
  that comes with the years, that is so sorrowful and blue.
The sun touches the mountains. It's getting colder.
  The light has a secret beauty. How beautiful is the vapory sun!
  Tell me that she cannot possibly lie there much longer.
It's getting critical. It's getting time for me to get on the road.
  My eyes, they are well on their way to turning into dust,
  and are damned near worthless
  for driving home in the dark.

LEARNING THE ALPHBET

My father had a very fat sister who was not only fat of body
but also fat of personality. As a kid, I lived in fear of her.
I trembled at the mere thought of having to be in her presence.
If I were to show any behavior not in keeping with what
she considered proper for a boy my age, one of her fat hands
would come flying, and with aim deadly and alarming, it would
deliver a powerfully shocking blow to the back of my head.
Okay, so that kind of experience was not all that endearing but,
if truth be told, my memories of her are not totally lacking
in gratitude (as icily tainted as that gratitude might prove to be).
I am very grateful to her for having taught me the alphabet.
I was in kindergarten when this remarkable event took place.
My parents, having little patience, had long ago thrown in the towel.
I'd begin reciting, but somewhere in the shaky neighborhood
of the letter G my mind would go ruthlessly blank and I'd have to start
all over again, only to achieve the same blankness. So,
it was decided that daily, after school, I should go to my aunt's house
until I could give a flawless performance of the entire alphabet.
She would sit me down at her kitchen table and I would recite
while she ate from a giant bag of potato chips. As I watched,
in disbelief and horror, her glossy lips grew fatter with cheap oil.
She'd lick her salty fingers as they kept going in and out
of the bag, pulling out one unfortunate chip after another,
stuffing them into her mouth. I would hear chips being pulverized,
being turned into mush that was then swallowed by her fat thick neck
that supported a head that had a face that had an expression that had
the confidence of a sperm whale devouring an octopus that had wanted
simply to be left alone, hugging the bottom of the ocean.
Day after day I'd recite without success, choking on letters. Mercilessly
this continued on, until it got to the point where I just couldn't
stomach the sight of her eating another chip, and finally, flawlessly I aced
the alphabet from A to Z. Not that this, mind you, earned me a
single potato chip as reward, but it did free me from having to be
at her table every afternoon after school. It was while I was in high school
that death came to her in the night. Her heart, I was told,
had simply quit pumping. It had quit when she was unaware
of the fact that it was quitting. Perhaps, we surmised,
her heart had been afraid of quitting while she was awake.
Perhaps, we further surmised, her heart had been afraid
of that fat voice accusing it and berating it and cursing it
for loafing on the job. That voice, that godawful fat voice
that had taught me the alphabet
without uttering a single word.

A HORSE'S FRONT TOOTH

There was a time, not long before my father died,
when he used to show up at the house here, unexpected.
This was when I was living alone, after a hellish breakup
with a woman I had been living with for seven years.
He'd pull in the driveway in his white Honda, parking within inches
of the garage door. He'd pound on the door and when I let him in
he'd stand there in the living room, looking at me as though I were
insane for being home. He'd never fail to ask me where my car was.
I'd tell him it was in the garage. He'd ask me why it was in the garage
and I'd tell him it was in there because I didn't want anybody to know
that I was home. He'd ask me if I was keeping all the lights off at night.
If it was evening, I'd remind him that it'd be getting dark soon,
and that maybe he shouldn't be driving in the dark. He'd pace.
Never once did he sit down. Like an old lion he'd pace, carrying
huge pain in his eyes, huge questioning pain, and he'd be mumbling
through lips thin and pale, lips having returned to what
they had been when he was a child. I knew his childhood lips,
especially from the one photograph of him standing next to his mother
when he was about five. She was enormous and grim looking,
a woman of intimidating presence which seems to make him very proud.
According to my father, she'd never hesitate to tell you
to go shit in your hat. My father would pace, complaining that
he had lived long enough, that he was tired of living, that he was
again contemplating suicide. I'd ask him how he intended to do this, and
he'd answer me by simply staring out a window. Before leaving
he'd never forget to look at the plaster ceiling, that had a big dip in it, and
he'd warn me that it was about to cave in. After he died, a small piece
of plaster did come loose and fall to the floor. It was about the size of
a horse's front tooth.
But so far, that's been it.

THE UNTOLD STORY

My intention was to keep the story simple,
but after a number of tellings I found myself

elaborating too much, to the point where
the original story somehow had gotten lost. So then

I just stopped telling the story. I stopped
telling it to myself, or even thinking about it.

Then, one night, the story came to me in a dream,
completely renewing the obsession I had with it.

Everything else in my life lacked importance,
was put on hold, and it got to the point where

I had to tell the story to someone, anyone, if only
as a way of forever ridding myself of it. I was afraid,

though, that I would again start elaborating, causing
gross distortions. What could I do but write it down.

Unfortunately, as soon as I began to do this
the sentences turned into complete strangers.

In despair I put my pen down and closed my notebook.
This story, I was resigned to admit, would remain untold.

After all, it's not as though the world would miss it.
The world only knows the stories it has been told.

I CANNOT READ WILLIAMS TONIGHT

I cannot read Williams tonight, but I can read Parra.
  Williams seems like a stranger while Parra is like
  a friend who has come to drink and spend the night.
On some other night the opposite might be true.
  On some other night Parra might be the stranger
  and Williams the good neighbor who has stopped by
for a brief visit, to talk about a locust tree or a yellow chimney.
  But tonight I want to listen to Parra talk about being an old man.
  I want him to tell me how an old man should eat chicken,
how he should hold the bones. Or, I would like to know
  how to get someone to massage an old man's feet without
  having to pay for it. Should an old man living alone
have a dog? Should the dog be old, also? Would it be better if
  the dog were to die first? If it did, how deep should an old man dig
to bury his old dog? As an old man, Parra would probably not risk
having a heart attack by digging a grave. Maybe
  he would leave the dog on someone's doorstep and walk away laughing.
  I would ask him if it is fair for an old man to hope that all
the bleak shadows of the compromises he has made through the years
  can also be left someplace, and if he could sneak off without them.
  Only, in this case, would the shadows do all the laughing?
I would ask him how an old man can look back, with any reasonableness,
  on the women he has loved and who have loved him.
  But of course I would not expect much in the way of an answer.
Parra could tell me if an old man ever gets used to pissing in his pants,
  if he gets used to the piss trickling down his legs, and whether
  he should celebrate if a warm yellow drop
successfully reaches one of the socks.
  What I don't need to be told is that either you are young or you are old,
  that there is no in-between. That one day
you have a spring in your step, and the next
  a dagger sending an onslaught of pain up into your skull.
  I don't need to be told that when you are old
the moon becomes even less poetic and encouraging.
  That it becomes some desolate object that has been
  following you around all your life, that you have been
senselessly staring at, all your life.

THE RIVER ROAD HOUSE

It was Marquez, I'm sure now, who said that when you go back
to the place of your childhood, nostalgia causes everything to appear
much smaller than what you remember. I certainly found this to
be the case when, one day, I went back to see the house on River Road
where I spent most of my childhood years. I sat in my car
on the other side of the road, staring at the house, befuddled
at how a family of five had managed ever to survive in such a
small space. I wondered why I had ever complained when
I had to mow the lawn. It couldn't have taken me more than
fifteen minutes to complete this chore. If the front lawn
had been a cemetery, it would have been able to accommodate,
at most, the burial of a string quartet, without their instruments.
True, as a kid I was very much aware that that kitchen was where
claustrophobia had originally sunk its big steel nails deep into me.
There's a photo showing our family sitting around the table, along
with visiting relatives, and it is just pathetic to see how we were all
so squashed together and on top of one another. The photo makes us
look as though we were trying to break the record for how many people
can sit around one miserable little table. How did that table ever hold
enough food to feed such a rowdy and famished crowd?
My father did manage to have a garden in the back yard. Not one
you could compare to the gardens he had later on in life
after he had retired and moved to a larger piece of land.
His first gardens grew nothing more than cucumbers and tomatoes.
From my curtained bedroom window, I would watch him
toiling away evenings after he had returned from his job.
My father was the spitting image of George Raft, the movie star whose
career spanned many decades. Raft was the quintessential gangster.
When I saw my father digging in his small garden, to me it looked like
he was digging a grave where he planned dumping the body of someone
he had bumped off. Perhaps it had been the very necessary murder
of a man who had simply never learned to keep his mouth shut. So,
my god, there I sat, staring at the house of minutest of joys, the house
of sorrow stricken years, the house that had sent forth the first green
sprouts of love. I could not help but marvel at the weird and cold
and blueful mysteries of consciousness. And I wasn't unaware of how
fortunate we had been, to have a strong roof over our heads, food
that was crammed and piled and ceaselessly passed around. And
there was the sublime chaos of relatives who never seemed to mind
bashing elbows while eating. But o, the River Road house, o it was
so unspeakably small and faceless. It looked like a mausoleum for
small birds.

BURIED ANIMALS

I'm praying that the bird doesn't die.
It stands there at the bottom of the cage

and it hasn't moved in two long days.
Only last week I buried the yellow cat

that should have lived another ten years.
Its grave has a covering of dead leaves.

You'd never know anything is buried there.
If the bird dies, I'll have to dig a new grave

and bury it next to the cat and then replace
the leaves. I won't replace the cat or the bird.

I am sick of weeping and digging new graves.
Two dogs lie buried next to the shed and there are

three more birds buried over by the rose bushes.
When I have it in me to move away, I will not return

to visit the graves of these animals that have left me.
People will come after me and they will not know

of the many animals that are buried behind this house.
They will come with their own animals, and they will bury

these animals when they are dead, and in the act of doing so
they will dig up the bones of my birds, my dogs and my cats,

all that had been wrapped in old blankets or handkerchiefs.
Perhaps the children will have fun playing with these bones.

Perhaps they will turn the bones into toys, maybe even weapons.
Perhaps in the hands of an imaginative child a bone will become

a spoon for eating dirt. Or a boomerang that doesn't come back.

MRS. EDDY

At night, in bed, I'd get my binoculars out and I'd part the curtains.
My neighbors were Mr. and Mrs. Eddy, and Mrs. Eddy was a very
attractive woman, at least from what I could tell in my boyhood.
Wherever she went, she wobbled on high heels, and her eyes were forever
popping out of her head, as though she were a fish being passionately
squeezed to death. She was never without a cigarette. Every night,
wearing a slip, she'd wobble around in a cloud of smoke in her kitchen
that was about the size of a small room in a motel. Her health was bad,
although I cannot recall what it was that ailed her. Periodically
an ambulance would roll up to their house and take her away.
They had a son, the Eddys did, but he never seemed to pay them a visit.
Back then, to help get through college, I had worked as a waiter in
a country club (a bitter education in itself). One day I showed Mrs. Eddy
a gold cigarette lighter I had found at the club, and which I had never
reported finding. Well, before I knew what happened, Mrs. Eddy
had snatched the lighter from my hands and had dropped it into the
pocket of her jacket, as though I had given it to her. What was I to do?
I didn't smoke and I liked Mrs. Eddy a lot, so I let her have it. Maybe
I had intended to give it to her all along. Considering she had given me
countless nights of pleasure, the least I could do was make a present
of something I had no use for anyway. But it wasn't long before
childhood melted away like a brief snowfall and the old obsessions
held little weight anymore. And, if I'm remembering correctly,
before I moved out of my parents' house for good, the Eddys decided to
go into hiding (what I thought an old person moving to Florida was doing)
for their remaining years. We never saw them again, but Mrs. Eddy
did write, and it seemed every one of those gold bordered letters
never failed to express regrets for having moved. The Eddys missed
the huge yard for their dogs to run around in (they always had dogs)
and the lawn which Mr. Eddy so meticulously took care of.
But, most of all, in a very lyrical and sentimental manner,
Mrs. Eddy expressed missing what living in a trailer park
would never be able to offer her in a million years, so she lamented.
She missed her sense of privacy.

SUDDENLY A WARM DAY

Suddenly a warm day, and before leaving the house this morning
  I notice a spider has constructed a web in the bedroom window
  between panes of glass, and the thought comes to me that, my god,
this spider must be daft or something. What with all this cold weather,
  I cannot imagine there being anything to trap. It is such an
  elegant web, too, so flawlessly designed, like a wavy silky blanket
on which the spider to its heart's content can walk back and forth.
  I stare at it; impressed, jealous even.
If only poetry would come to me with the same perfection and purpose.
I think it a shame that this web should go to waste. Yet
  when I return to the house in the afternoon I notice
  many small flies have fallen victim to this web. There are
a couple of wasps also near the web, but they seem capable
  of easily freeing themselves should they come in contact with it.
  I cannot help standing at the window, enjoying this little
nature show in October, fascinated with how a bit of warmth
  brings back all the old characters of summer. Even the katydids
  are making a beautiful racket. Unfortunately, this respite
from the cold will not last long. Soon, in freezing temperatures,
  the katydids will fall silent again, the wasps will be numbed
  into inactivity, the spider will pack it in and the remaining flies
will commit suicide.

NAKED WOMEN

We were maybe 7 or 8 when Michael and I started robbing candy stores.
We'd rob small things, nothing worth more than a couple of dollars.
We'd work as a team. Our favorite target was the store owned by
Sam Brown. Mr. Brown was old and he didn't know what was going on.
At first we restricted ourselves to candy, but as we grew bolder we
started stealing magazines, Playboy to be precise. And so, life
took on new meaning, one fraught with much sweetness and danger.
After leaving the store with one of these magazines, we'd cut through
the woods and come out where there was an abandoned factory.
And it was there that we felt safe enough to stop and open the magazine,
and when we did our eyes became big as golf balls. At first
our greedy hands would fight over the magazine, but then, just
as suddenly, a wordless truce was struck and our hands would begin
to work in harmony to reveal unbelievable picture after picture.
I don't think we actually had any idea of what we were gawking at.
We had no idea of what took place between a man and a woman,
of what the ultimate goal was that mother nature had in mind.
All we knew, was that we were helpless before the ravishing creatures
on the glossy pages, and we didn't ask any questions. Besides,
who were we going to ask, each other? When we had finally curbed
our enthusiasm over the magazine, we would continue our walk home
in a state of giddy ecstasy. In the pure blue light of a boyhood summer,
we were oblivious to the endless havoc and treacheries that existed
between the sexes. Conversely, we were unaware of how the love
of a woman could save a man's life. We were blissfully ignorant of this
and a lot more. The only vital concern facing us was the question of
who would get to take the magazine home with him. One time, we got
into such a bitter argument over this that we tore the magazine in half,
Michael getting the bottom half of the centerfold and I the top.
I remember feeling very sorry for this woman. I felt as though
Michael and I had committed a sacrilege. I wasn't able to see this
as the grim foreshadowing that it was, of all the trouble and heartache
I was destined to cause women in the years to come. That night
I thought about Michael lying in his bed, with his half of
the stolen magazine hidden between the mattress and the box spring.
I had done the same with my half. And every night
it was mandatory that I kneel at the side of the bed and say my prayers.
Naturally, when I'd be in the middle of performing this ritual
I couldn't take my mind off the many naked women stuffed in my bed.
And whenever my mother caught me kneeling there and
playing with myself, she'd become furious and warn me that
if I persisted in this habit my penis would turn into a fish.
After a number of such warnings, I couldn't help asking her
what kind of fish was it that she was talking about.
She looked at me with very serious, very watery eyes, and
she said, "A sardine." I then asked her if that included both
a head and a tail, and with that she left the room to go in search
of my father. Within moments he came into my bedroom and
sat down on the bed and said, "Son, don't ask your mother such
stupid questions." As I looked up at him sitting there, on top of

all those naked women, including the woman that had been torn in half, I couldn't help wondering whether his penis had a head and a tail.

I figured it wouldn't hurt asking. Also, I wanted to know if a sardine could see in the dark.

THIS SUNLIGHT

I remember
this sunlight
from childhood.
This was the sunlight
of long summers.
Of the black river
on the other side
of the narrow road.
Of the small garden
crowded with tomatoes.
Of the birds that came for
the shrinking orange berries.
This was the sunlight
of all the early sorrows.
Of happiness
resilient as grass.
Of a book left
in a hot car.

THE MOON IS A FRIEND
FROM THE OLD COUNTRY

The more years I experience life
on this insane lovely little blue planet,
the more I've come to realize that I am

a creature nocturnal to the bone.
I thrive in the bliss of sheer darkness,
and if I could I would sleep the days away.

When the sun is overhead I feel exposed
and doomed, as though trapped with a hyena
in a cage. Whereas the moon is like a friend

from the old country. Instead of worshipping
the sun, I'd prefer simply to watch a motorcycle
approaching on a lonesome highway. Instead of

getting a suntan, I'd rather descend the stairs
to the cellar with flashlight in hand so that I can
see what's what with the fuses. The sun interrogates.

The moon serenades. The moon is a glass of cold milk
from one of those hot summer days in childhood. And,
my god, all those gloriously harmless stars, I cannot help

but enjoy watching them spinning in the night sky.
All those suns at such a safe distance; the bunch
of them cannot light a path in the dark woods.

It is best to simply make love by starlight and
forget the gnawing responsibilities of daylight.
Yes, make love at night and the hell with the sun!

YOU HAVE TURNED ME INTO
A SENTIMENTAL OLD GOAT

You have turned me into a sentimental old goat
and there seems little I can do about it.
I was fine with the thought of the years serenely

dwindling away and that out in the tomato garden
death was patiently waiting for me. I had my
suspicions, I admit, that its patience was wearing thin, that it

was getting anxious to take advantage of me, maybe on some
hot suffocating afternoon when I might be caught
unaware while weeding out in the garden. Or, it could be

that it has been considering stealing into my bedroom,
at night when I am drunk and asleep, to slip
through my ribs, to apply that final, quietly devastating

stranglehold to my heart. But now, my dearest sweetness,
that I am sleeping with you, my god, perhaps death has
decided, hopefully, to give this sentimental old goat

a few more precious years. It's rare, but even death
sometimes thinks twice about being so rude as to
come between two lovers, especially two who have

just recently found one another so late in life. This
is an extremely rare occurrence, though, as I said.
As we know, death will intrude, with the drop of the

biggest black hat imaginable, upon the happiest of lives.
On mere whim alone it could snatch one of us right out
of our bed, separating us on the most passionate of nights.

Naturally, now that I am possessed by this great blessing
that is your love, I do not want death anywhere near me.
I do not want its fingers to brush over my skin. I do not want

to smell its breath, which is repulsive. I do not want
its nose smelling my inner organs. It should rot, death should,
in my tomato garden, and it should come back to life

in some other old man's garden. Some old man who is alone and
bored and filled with self-pity, and who would welcome,
with open arms, the sudden companionship

of death.

THIS GENTLE RAIN

Other than the rain, the only sound
is the cawing of a crow. It's almost
as though this crow is complaining
about the rain, which has been falling
throughout most of the day now.
It is the tail end of what has been
a very destructive hurricane. Now
it can barely lift the bedroom curtains.
It moves leaves with such innocence,
as though not having been responsible
for so much mayhem and death.
This gentle rain sounds more like
the storm simply washing its hands
of any guilt.

ANOTHER TEN MINUTES

For me, March will always be the month during which my father died.
I like to think it's not the worst month to die in, especially
for a man like my father who lived to spend every last waking moment
in his garden. In March, the earth is barren and unresponsive.
Perhaps it isn't an overly sad month to leave it. Surely it would be
more difficult to die on a beautiful day in summer, or on a spring day
of warm and promise-giving breezes. Even in autumn, when death
is everywhere and the nights are growing cold, even then the world is
too sublime with glorious resignation to allow departure to be easy.
And who would want to miss those first fires and the joy of the holidays
(what little joy is left). But we do not have much say in these matters.
When a person's time is up (as they say), it's up. We all know this.
Most of us will admit this with a shrug of nonchalant indifference.
As for myself, since childhood I've had the eerie suspicion that I will
die in August. Perhaps the cause will be nothing more than what
Conrad called the tragic brutalities of daylight. But, why would I be
so sure of the month and not the year? Well, of course, to know the year
would be intolerable. And, if death does come to me in August, then
early morning would be preferable, after a decent night's sleep and when
the air is still cool and the sheets still desirable. The window being open
would be fine, with birds singing in the elegantly twisted old apple tree.
I'd prefer to die alone, without another soul's tearful eyes riveted to me.
At the moment of death I'd like to let loose with one last big fart, and
feel as though I'm simply turning over to sleep another ten minutes.

EGG SANDWICHES

I drink a glass of wine and then
after my mother and I have the
usual conversation I stretch out
on the couch with my notebook.
I scribble a page before falling off
to sleep. When I wake, I see my mother,
frail and bent over, eating a piece of
toast in bright sunlight flowing through
the window facing the garden that has
disappeared since my father's death.
It seems she is returning to the shape
of a fetus. What can I put down on paper
to record even a glimpse of her inner life?
I feel helpless, and what is far worse
is that other than sleeping and scribbling
on the couch, I do nothing around the house.
Another woman comes to the house to do
cleaning and shopping. There is a handyman
who is hired to do whatever needs to be done.
He charges by the hour. He has found reason to
cut down many of the trees surrounding the house,
trees I would've judged healthy and having many
more beautiful years ahead of them. But, if I say
anything regarding such matters, I'm ignored.
After all, I am simply the lazy poet son who is
good for little else than brief conversations,
drinking wine, musing, eating an egg sandwich
and snoozing. Over the years my mother has made
for me numberless egg sandwiches filled with such
warmth and love that I always felt as though I were
eating pure sorrow. She fell again, recently but,
fortunately, she didn't break anything. At 89,
chances are she won't survive another broken hip.
This time she fell while out feeding the birds.
From the fall she has had pains that were making her
cranky and pessimistic. But earlier, when she was
preparing my egg sandwich, I realized, with great relief,
she was successfully on the mend. After she sneezed
I heard her say to herself, "They're getting better,
the sneezes, not as ugly, they don't hurt anymore."

DIALOGUE OF THE ROCKS

Again I find myself driving to the river in a mood
  to waste time and perhaps, if lucky, to scribble a haiku.
  Usually I'll walk until I come to the closed bridge.
The water is calm and I am able to rummage through
  and inspect many rocks. I find one that is round and smooth,
  the size of a grapefruit, and I cradle it in my hands.
I notice rock sculptures on the other side of the river.
  I'm drawn to creating the same. Such sculptures possess
  a simplicity and directness that I would like to capture in my writing.
Often I'll build one with the hope of learning a little something
  from the experience. On this occasion, though, I do so in order
  to have a dialogue with the person responsible for the sculptures
on the other side of the river. A light rain starts to fall matter-of-factly.
  The rocks appear immaculate and highly polished and I want
  to take them home with me. I fondle one as if it were my consciousness.
I press my nails into it, questioning its existence. But, in an attempt
  to reshape, elevate and impart to it some marvelous air of immortality,
  my inability is unquestionable and I place the rock back in the
cold rushing water where it belongs. Instead, I create a pile of rocks that
  comes up to my chin and which appears earnest and serene;
  I like to think it speaks my mind, even though I know it will not last long,
that rising water will cause it to tumble in ruins, or another
  wandering soul will come along and destroy it. The compulsion
  to destroy is as natural and powerful as the act of creation.
Who will deny that at times nature's delicate balancing act
  can prove to be downright infuriating? I return to my car, to
  my notebook and fountain pen so I can scribble a haiku
that has been fluttering about the dim light in my mind.
  It has nothing to do with the piling of rocks by the river.
  Instead, it is about the grapefruit eaten at breakfast. It's wonderful
the way the haiku flows without pause from my fountain pen.
  And it's no surprise to see a drop of rain fall from
  the bill of my baseball cap
that utterly destroys this haiku.

SURRENDER TO THE LAMB

Embrace violent laughter
Accept skinny chickens
Pray the worn dark beads
Slice the perfect peach
Ride the heavenly mule

Cream the anxious coffee
Paint the red wagon red
Swallow the friendly pea
Lasso the slowest pony
Squirt the angel of death

Question the arrogant monkey
Dip the reluctant sugar cone
Adore the slightest suspicion
Make sacred the green beetle
Suckle bliss from evening's wine

Smile at the brazen accusation
Pamper the frozen rose
Kiss the beggar's cup
Ignore the fear of cliffs
Skip over stones of fury

Buy every luminous fish
Rent a monstrous picnic basket
Pressure the wounded to go home
Retrieve what's in front of you
Loosen what chokes the tulip

Fondle the dancer's old shoes
Respect time's indifference
Squeeze the wandering beauty
Climb to the top of the slightest whim
Surrender to the lamb.

EINSTEIN SAID

Einstein said his first wife had the soul of a herring.
Naturally when I read this I began to wonder what
my first wife would say my soul most resembled.
Believe me, I'd be greatly relieved if, in one of her
more generous and kinder moments, she said
my soul had at least the worth of a kitchen canary.
I've always admired how well this bird adapts
to being forced to dwell in a room made witness
to many of the obvious and not so obvious
worryings of everyday life. Somehow its
song continues sweet and uncomplicated.

A RAINY NIGHT AND I DREAM
OF HER FEET AGAIN

A rainy night and I dream of her feet again, or
  I should say that the dream I have of her feet wakes me
 and I become aware of rain falling on the roof with a fine precision.
I listen, and I'm convinced that this sound would make any
  perfectionist green with envy. In my dream, her feet had the
 reassuring fragrance of geraniums thriving in a hot house in winter,
and they were gentle when walking across my chest, the thin, flimsy
  platform that it is. Or, perhaps, it was the sheer loveliness of her feet
 in my dream that woke me, the sadness of such loveliness.
Without question, the same exact sadness stalks time.
  It is the loveliness of her feet which causes me to fear my own death,
  when there will be no more feeling in my chest and I will have nothing
to say about the fate of such loveliness. I cannot tolerate the thought of
  another man taking her feet in his hands to massage comfort into them,
 or, worse, god forbid, if he were to place his miserable lips upon her feet.
From my grave I will haunt any man who attempts to do this.
  I will keep him awake and cause him the worst
 pounding headaches on his most drunken nights.

O BLESSED HORNS

In a dream I see my dead father standing in his garden in winter.
And in this dream he has wings long as the wings of an angel
and as reliable as the wings of a sparrow. These wings, they remain

perfectly still and draped down his back as he stares at the ground.
The sky is a cold, dark, austere gray and there is the look of snow
in the air but not a flake is falling. I want to call out to him.

I want to call out to urge him to leave his garden. I want to tell him
that his days in the garden are over, that the garden will be no more
because, you father, are of this earth no more. Even though I know

he knows this better than I, still, I feel I must give him what
encouragement I can. I want to call out and let him know I am here,
but my voice falters and is of no use. His wings remain as still

as marble cliffs. And my voice is as quiet as the worms he so
depended on to help tend the soil. But there is the sound of horns,
I swear. I hear these horns as you would hear the wind, or as

you would not hear the wind. I hear them, o sweet choir of horns,
encouraging him to use his wings. Horns! O blessed horns!
Between the dead and wherever the dead are fated to travel, there is

no other sound that rejoices and laments with such arousing clarity.
There is no other sound that summons and welcomes with such
embracing conviction. I watch my father bend to put his fingers

into the dark soil. I see him lift this soil to his nose, pause
in recognition and longing, then throw it over his shoulder
as though it were a pinch of salt. Finally, cautiously, his

wings move, resigned to the truth of their mission. Wings
long as the wings of an angel, reliable as those of the sparrow.
Wings to release him from the overwhelming and from the

very common sorrow of leaving.

JUST REST

just rest
don't think
of anything

just rest
under leaves
falling and

just rest
under shadows
falling too

don't think
don't concern
yourself at all

with this aloneness
that has come
as it has always

don't shed any
tears or toss
and turn

don't attempt
trying to see or
trying to understand

nothing will come of it
and only valuable
sleep will be lost

just rest
don't think
of anything

let the leaves
fall and let them
bury you.

THE STICKBALL BAT

We'd play stickball at the far end of the field where
  there was a wall very suitable to draw a strike zone
  on with chalk. We'd stay out until called in for dinner.
One morning, when my friends came to the house to
  drag me away from the breakfast table, they told me
  there was no bat to be had, that the bat we had used
the day before had disappeared and that if we didn't
  come up with a new one then there would be no
  stickball games that day. They all looked at me as though
I were the one responsible for supplying the new bat.
  As it turned out, I did just that. I went into the garage and
  I took one of my father's rakes and I sawed off the handle.
I sawed it off so it would be the length of a bat; what was
  remaining of the rake I simply put back where the whole rake
  had once been. It didn't take long for my father to discover
one of his rakes was without a handle. Naturally, after finding
  the tragic remains of his rake, he immediately came to me
  for an explanation. What could I do but play dumb,
which was the only natural gift I had been born with.
  I looked at him as though he were asking me a question that
  there was no way on God's green earth I could ever answer.
He knew I was lying. He knew there was no one else who
  would ever dream of destroying a perfectly good rake. But
  I held my ground, and by the time he was done cross-examining me
I believed what I was saying. I believed that I was not capable
  of committing such a hideously inconsiderate and selfish act.
  I was not the kind of person who would stoop so low as to destroy
a tool that my father cherished and took such very good care of.
  After all, this was the man who, when there was a water shortage,
  had gone into the garage, to the far end of it, and started digging.
After work and on weekends he dug and shoveled, dug and
  removed countless wheelbarrows of dirt until one day, triumphantly,
  he succeeded in digging a well. He had dug a well so that
he could water his lawn, but also he had dug a well so that
  my younger sister's plastic blue pool could have water in it every day.
  This being the very same pool in which I had attempted to drown her
Raggedy Ann doll.

TANGLED HAIR

From the bed, I watch as she combs her tangled hair.
  As she works at it she talks about the plans that
  have to deal with what will happen after breakfast.
When she finally stops untangling her hair, there is a fine hint
  of breathy ecstasy in her voice, as entering through
  the bedroom window there is light, beaming and yellow.
It seems to be offering assurances that there certainly is
  a good chance that life can be lived well enough
  before we once again make our return to the bed.
But a disturbance in the air forbids complete stillness to every hair.
  One in particular floats up from her head, catching the light
  with striking and unexpected precision. And, somehow,
almost miraculously, without mirror, she knows what is happening
  to this hair, and with two fingers she captures it and brings it down
  and places it exactly where she thinks it belongs.
She does this while suggesting that I make breakfast,
  as though her deft handling of the one hair has somehow,
  unquestionably, freed her from this chore.

SUMMERS AT THE LAKE

As a child, I spent summers in a cabin by a lake
  which was surrounded by nothing but other cabins.
  There was a restriction on motorboats, so the peaceful atmosphere
was rarely interrupted. Most importantly, there was no television,
  so we were forced to occupy ourselves in other ways. One day
  I found some books at the bottom of a cedar chest, safely tucked away
underneath heavy blankets. It was a collection of great literature, each
  book infused with the scent of cedar. And so, I started
  with Treasure Island and I made my way through what was there.
Often I'd take a book out in the rowboat and read
  while waves lapped up against the side of the boat. Or
  mornings, I'd read while lying in bed. If I put the book down
I could see the lake reflected on the sky-blue ceiling.
  At night I'd read on the back porch, and if I put the book down
  while out there I could see lights reflecting on the lake's blackness.
Sometimes I'd take a book and a box of stick matches and go off
  into the woods, where I'd sit on a large rock in the center of the stream.
  If I grew tired of reading I'd light one stick match after another,
throwing them into the rushing water where they'd make a hissing sound,
  and eventually they would be carried out of sight.
When there were no more stick matches,
  I'd go back to reading.

ACCORDING TO MY MOTHER

According to my mother, my grandmother used to dry mushrooms
  by hanging them on a string over the stove.
  When her feet were tired and sore she would sit in her
rocker with her feet almost under the stove.
  She believed it was bad luck to use scissors on Sunday,
  that it was good luck to put walnuts under the kitchen table.
My own memories of my grandmother are not many.
  As a child I saw her, at most, once or twice a year.
  I never looked forward to the big wet kiss she would plant on my face
when greeting me on that long front porch. I don't know
  how old she was when she came to this country.
  Supposedly, she met my grandfather on the boat.
He died before I was born. She looked like a true old world peasant.
  I never spoke to her because she did not speak English.
  No effort was ever made to help me understand her language.
I picked up a handful of words, one being the word for potato.
  Another was a one-syllable word that expressed fatigue from the sorrows
  of everyday life. In her eighties, my mother is far more attractive
than my grandmother was at that age. My grandfather
  was a remarkably handsome man, and I suspect it was from him
  that my mother got her good looks. Perhaps my grandfather
had to marry my grandmother. Maybe he had gotten her pregnant
  on the boat to America. No doubt it had been a long and tedious and
  boring journey. And maybe lovers were able to gain moments of privacy
now and then, preferably at night and if the ocean was calm and seductive.
  The heavy breathing of the other passengers
  would have been a rich and exquisite blend of fear and hope.

OF LATE

I've been
terminating
relationships

it scares me
it started with
one person

and now it has
spread to others
where will it

end
as it is
I've seen no one

in weeks
my phone bill
should be

embarrassingly
low
at least no one

will see it
I eat alone
I drink alone

I hold up both ends
of a conversation
I kill only

one
very small bird
for dinner

MY RELIGION

I see myself an old man living by the ocean,
painting watercolors, and if I'm lucky
selling them for maybe five dollars each.
The money I could put towards food and wine.
Poetry has always been worthless.
It has been my religion, yes, one I am thankful for.
But religions and gods come and go
and still you have to eat and drink.

THE PROMISE

the irises by the
garage are
blooming

the same yellow
faint as that of
onion skins

I should cut some
and take them
to my old neighbor

who was not so old
ten years ago
when I came here

to live
but a strange illness
I can never remember

the name of
has stolen every last
vestige of youth from her

one hot august afternoon
while we were standing in
the shade of her back porch

she had made me promise
never to grow old
and to bring a smile to her face

I promised I'd do my best.

LEAVING

Leaving, I can plainly see that my mother's eyes are sad.
When your mother is very old, and you are leaving,
your mother's eyes will always be sad. They will be sad
and worried because you are returning to the world
which she is no longer a part of. If my mother should die
before I do, I hope she comes to me in a dream.
I hope she has a pear in one hand and a rose in the other.
The pear she will give to me and the rose she will keep
for herself. The pear will be ripe; the rose will be yellow
and without thorns.

EATING STARS

After my mother died I had a number of dreams about her.
  I feared having these dreams. I thought they
 would mercilessly enhance the sorrow that already
haunted my days. But when the dreams arrived they proved
  to be very consoling. I saw my mother floating in
 a horizontal position over the woodstove, that was in the kitchen
of the house where she spent her childhood years. In one dream,
  in fact, she was a child. She was about five years of age and in
 her arms she held a large bouquet of various kinds of wildflowers.
Her father lay on the floor, curled up next to the woodstove
  for warmth, using his hands joined in prayer for a pillow.
 I could hear music being played by what sounded like
a piccolo quartet. It was sublime and gentle, but
  at the same time very exhilarating. And I remember thinking,
 in this dream, that I had never heard music in a dream before.
There was a large black iron pot on the woodstove and
  steam was rising from it. Eventually the figure of my mother
 became suffused with this steam, until she became indistinct
and she floated out the window. I saw her rise above the house
  and leave the hillside the house was situated on, and then
 the village the hillside was situated in, and then
the luscious green country the village was situated in, and then
  the pearly blue planet the country was situated in.
 She left behind the prayers of this planet, its
merriment and its murders. And her father smiled
  in his sleep, as the chickens in the yard smiled
  at the stars, fully intending to peck their way
towards them,
  to eat them.

GOD AND THE FLIES

I miss the god of my childhood.
I hope to live long enough to recover
this precious intimacy. Who knows
what might occur in my decaying brain.
It will resemble a temple in ruins.
But even with all its statues gone
it might still be a welcome place
to live out my remaining time.
I imagine that on most days
there might be little else to do
than sweep up the dead flies.

OUTSIDE FOREVER

I visit my mother at the nursing home.
She tells me her mother and her sisters
had visited earlier in the day.

She tells me this after I take her outside
in her wheel chair, while we are sitting
by a garden of many yellow flowers.

I have never noticed this before, that
all the flowers are yellow, and when I
mention this to my mother she says

that of course she knows this. Blind
and ravaged by the loss of memory,
she casually says this.

Her struggle is unrelenting, and for brief
periods of time she is aware that her brain
is not functioning as it should be. She

questions me. She wants to know what
is happening to her. I do not have it
in me to tell her that when a person is

nearing death, often that person will sense
the closeness of those loved ones who
are already numbered among the dead.

Is there anyone who thinks I should tell her?
Should I tell her she is dying? She does not
speak of dying. She speaks of living.

She asks how her cat Mooche is doing,
if the tomato plants have been watered,
if I have fallen and hurt myself recently,

if I have been sleeping well, if I have had
another dream of my father, if in my dream
he was in his garden weeding without

a hat on to protect himself from the sun.
She asks if I am being faithful to my wife.
I say nothing about death. I ask her about

her mother and her sisters. I give her
a chocolate kiss which she rolls around
in her mouth and sucks on and chews with

no teeth. She holds my hand and presses it
close to her face. She tells me she would
like to sleep outside, that when I leave

it would be okay if I left her where she is.
She wants to sleep with a breeze on her. She
wants to hear the cicadas and the trains at night.

She tells me she could stay outside forever.

SOME SIMPLE TRUTH

The stars seem larger this winter than in past winters.
They don't even look like the same stars, as though

the old ones were replaced by new ones which are
more robust and swirling. I would like to stay out here

in this snowy field but the intensity of the cold won't
permit me to. I'd like to stay out here and study these

heavenly bodies, discern which are suitable to pray to
and which deserving to be cursed at. I feel like an

old scrawny ignorant monkey gawking at the cosmos.
And, speaking of being an ignorant monkey in the face

of all that is beautiful and sublime and mysterious,
it's evident that every word I have scribbled in this

perplexing life was pure nonsense. But I have always
known this and I have, nonetheless, thrived, I suppose.

It was all no more important than pushing sand from
one place to another. If I had to choose between all

I've created with words and the ability to grow wings,
well, no doubt I would choose the wings. But perhaps

flying would be no less lonely than writing. Hopefully
separating myself from the earth, and all that goes with it,

with the power and elegance of wings larger than myself-
hopefully this would make for a joyful rush of liberation.

Geese and vultures would envy me. I would ascend higher
into the heavens than any bird. I would follow dawn

around the world and watch cities and canyons come
to light. In my state of freedom I would never fly too low

or sing songs in praise of myself. This would only
draw attention to me and my strangeness would

cause people to throw stones and launch rockets.
I would like to be mistaken for an angel. I would hope

to appear as some simple truth. But, as we all know,
no one would accept this truth. Maybe some

demented soul, out of sheer unclouded bliss, would
understand that I had once been a poet, a poet

who had once turned into a monkey which had then
grown wings, each larger than a cathedral door and

each the burnt orange color of the harvest moon.
And perhaps, perhaps maybe I would look like

an angel, after all, one cast not only out of heaven
but also out of hell.

Orange peels-
the shadows of them
as I remember
the shadows of them
curling in childhood.

www.ingramcontent.com/pod-product-compliance
Lightning Source LLC
Chambersburg PA
CBHW021336090426
42742CB00008B/622